im
I'm } perfect
No one is

imperfect

the spontaneous spiritual awakening of a suicidal addict

by jennifer ann butler

AQp
Aquarius Press

Aquarius Press

A Division of Aquarius Media Network

1027 McConnell Drive

Decatur, GA 30033

www.aquarius-atlanta.com

ISBN: 978-0-9909741-0-9

Printed in the United States of America

This is an incredibly honest account. Jen opens up to give the reader a very clear picture of some very private and often painful truths about her life.

You will also find joy in her triumphs.

Thank you to everyone who donated to bring this book to fruition.

HEART HUGS AND JAZZ HANDS OF THANKS TO:

Dad, for being my rock and for never—not once—judging me. Mom, for believing in every creative idea I've ever had ever. Chipper, for feeding me gourmet meals while I was in the hermit phase of writing. Don, for telling me to write this thing and holding my hand throughout the process. Sandy, for sticking by my side and loving all of me, especially the messy parts. Hailey, for seeing through my bullshit, being a bulldozer, and not being afraid of my walls. Tyler and Daniel, for standing up *to* me *for* me. And Andy, for teaching me about the many facets of love.

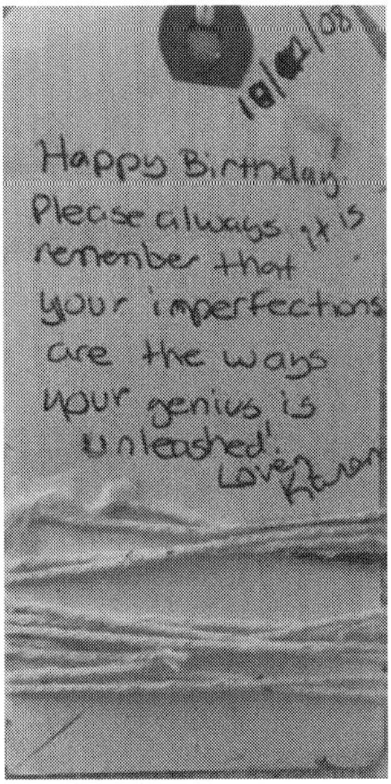
10/02/08
Happy Birthday!
Please always it is
remember that
your imperfections
are the ways
your genius is
unleashed!
Love,
Karen

Karen,

Thank you for helping me learn that it's okay to color outside of the lines. Even though you've left your earthly form, your passion lives on through the words of the students you inspired.

IT IS ALSO OKAY TO COLOR WITHIN THE LINES IF THAT IS WHERE YOU ARE COMFORTABLE.

this is the only sub-section title

A few things before we get started:

1. In my mom's honor, I have omitted the F word from this book. It was really lucking hard to do, but I trucking prevailed. (I love you, Mommy. I look forward to stuffed cabbage for Christmas.)
2. In order to help the energy of this book reach more people, it is imperative that it doesn't remain stagnant. So I ask (I kind of beg) that, when you are done reading these pages, you write a little love note in the back and you **put the book out in public. Or give it to a friend.** *I am a firm believer in universal alignment. Somehow, on the random Tuesday afternoon that you decide to go to the local coffee shop and leave this book under the singular open umbrella, there's gonna' be some person in the midst of a big ball of emotional angst who picks up the book and says, "Damn. This is exactly what I needed to read."* Since I chose self-publication, I am sort of relying on the flow state of this pay-it-forward approach to get this collection of imperfect words into more hands. Have fun.

   INDEED!

3. Please write on these pages. Make notes. In fact, I ask that you dog ear this page *just because.* My dream is that, by the time this specific copy reaches its 20th reader, it'll be a hot mess with doodles and notes in the margin and tears in the pages. So have at it. Make a mess.

   SORRY JEN, I JUST CAN NOT DOG EAR MAKES ME CRINGE

4. The general premise behind this book is that everyone needs a messy first time. A first book. A first on-stage performance. A first date. A first attempt at cooking tacos. It's all about taking that first step and allowing grace for muck-ups and imperfections. So, if you find inconsistencies or redundancies in this book? *Good.*

~ * ~

The wadded ball of hair stared at me from its perch on the edge of the bathtub. I moved closer and placed my chin a few inches away from it. I eyeballed its intricacies, unable to tell where one of my hairs ended and another began. I squinted in thought.

"I think you're what my insides look like," I said aloud.

I am, it responded.

"So how do I get untangled? I want to tell my story, but I don't know where to start."

Start somewhere. Anywhere. Gently pull and allow to unravel.

"But then it won't be linear. It won't make sense. It'll be messy."

Perfect, it said.

LET'S DO THIS.
ONE STRAND AT A TIME

The wisdom of this hairball has stuck with me since. The bath occurred about two months after I'd completely quit taking anti-depressants. As an expected result of discontinuing this medication, I came face-to-face with my depression and suicidality. This is something that was debilitating years ago. However, I've spent the last two years digging, healing, and retraining my brain in preparation for this chapter of my journey.

During another bath session within the same week—except this time fully clothed and with no water—I meditated with my journal and allowed stream of consciousness writing to flow through me and onto the page. What came through was that emotions are neither negative nor positive; they simply are. When judgment is removed from emotions, they can be seen for what they really are: *energy.*

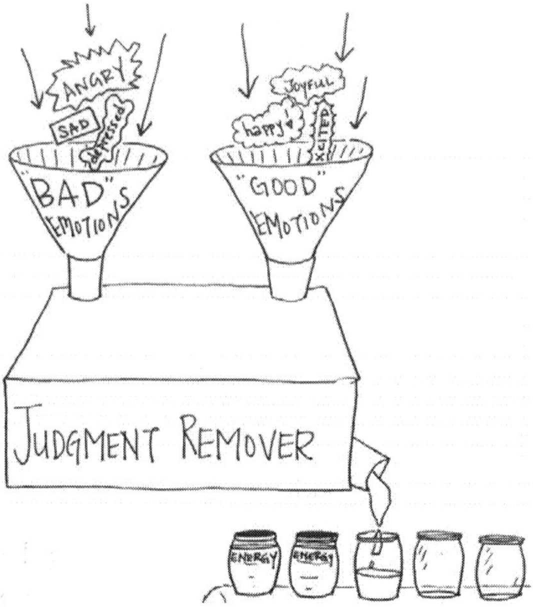

The next step, I was told, is to *use this energy as fuel.* When I asked what the vehicle would be, the written response was:

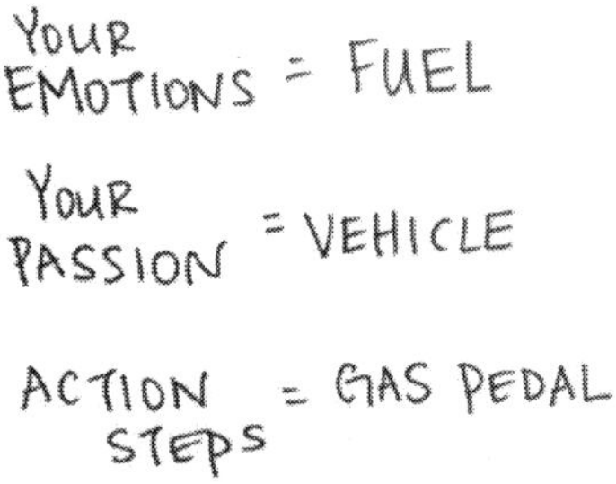

Being a visual person with a deep passion for doodles, I imagine the fueling process looks something like this:

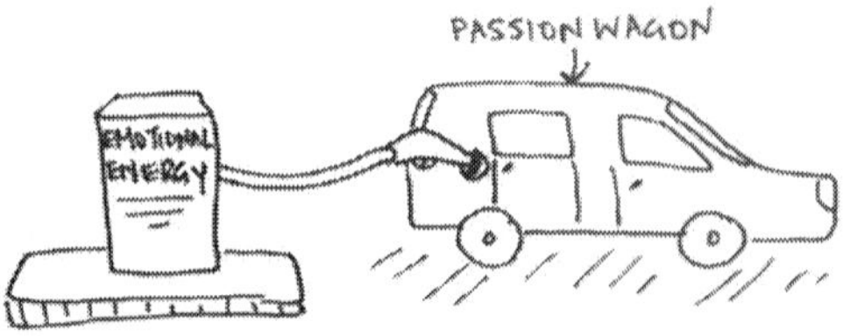

My next question to ask myself was: **WHAT AM I PASSIONATE ABOUT?** Removing the attached expectation of money or success or accolades, what do I adore doing? If I had all of the dollars I could ever need (and a wildly expansive sock collection as a result), what would I do? I would write. And I would doodle. And I would do inspirational speaking.

Yea, but… How the heck is something I enjoy THAT much going to bring me success?

Being particularly stubborn, skeptical, and fantastically talented at procrastinating, the hairball's wisdom and the bathtub's motivational speech still weren't quite enough to kick me into action for writing this book.

HOW TO WRITE THE BOOK:

- [x] 2 YEARS OF PERSONAL WORK
- [x] TALK TO HAIRBALL
- [x] LISTEN TO BATHTUB
- [ ] WATCH 1994 FLICK W/CHRISTOPHER LLOYD
- [ ] DOODLE A DRAGON
- [ ] READ BATHROOM MIRROR

This book has been tickling me for a long time, begging to be written. I've avoided it. I've tried to fit it into neat and tidy little boxes that I copied from other people's successful books under the silent belief that *in order to be successful, I must follow in the footsteps of successful people.* This resulted in my feeling frustrated, bored, annoyed, and confused. When trying to write a certain way, my creative juices go from grape to raisin within ten to twenty pages.

I journaled and meditated and prayed and the same guidance came through: *do something fun.*

Naturally, I ignored this guidance and instead chose to stress myself out over the book I *wasn't* writing. It's as though utilizing my chaotic creative energy toward my spinning thoughts gives me the illusion of accomplishment.

I eventually tried reading a fiction book as an attempt at this mystical idea of fun. (My comfortable state is one of hyper-seriousness and workaholism. "Fun" is a rather new concept for me that I've only recently incorporated into my life.) I thought maybe reading of a fictional world would bring me the inspiration I needed. It only took a few pages for me to grunt and [gently] throw the book.

I have read *one* fiction book in the last decade. Everything else has been for school, for work, or for self-improvement. The fiction book I attempted in this instance was gifted to me by a friend who said it'd be good for me to escape my mind every now and then. And I'm thinking, *Dude. I have detailed conversations with inanimate objects. My world is plenty of fun.*

Fiction and fun can be difficult journeys for me to embark upon. I get caught up in not knowing the point of such endeavors. This ties into the belief of "no pain, no gain." *How on earth can something enjoyable and imaginative assist me toward my dreams? That's preposterous.* That being said, once I dive in and awkwardly paddle a bit, I discover just how useful "useless" fun is. It's an experiential sort of thing; words can only go so far as to describe the effects of creative enjoyment.

One night, my roommate came home in a particularly bouncy mood. She had just completed one of her regular dates with the $5 movie bin at Walmart. The movie she brought home was:

Before I could formulate a response, the following words came out of my mouth: "Let's watch it."

"Now?" She asked, clearly excited.

"Yes," I said before thinking.

We settled into our usual movie-watching spots and pressed play. The flick stars Macaulay Culkin and Christopher Lloyd and is about a little boy (Culkin) who takes himself way too seriously and lives life paralyzed by fear of catastrophes. During a particularly scary storm, he hides out in a library. He ends up getting stuck, turning into a cartoon, and has to overcome his fears through the adventures of classic fiction books to return to real life.

Let's recap. I had received guidance to have fun. I had even been given fiction books to read. I had previously done lots of journaling and therapy on pushing through fear rather than remaining paralyzed by it. Still, I remained stuck and stagnant. Then, once Roommate and I watched a short flick about a fearful kid escaping into a creative world and overcoming scary obstacles, something clicked inside of me.

After the movie, I decided to doodle… For no other reason than to doodle. (This is admittedly hard for me to do. I like having *reasons* behind my actions. I prefer to be actively moving toward something in a linear way that my brain comprehends rather than something as seemingly pointless as "just because.") With zero preconceived expectations, here is what my hand created:

I had to look hard to see the dragon. We often see much more when we look closer.

My doodle gave me very clear guidance. It told me to create whatever my heart desired and to allow that creation to defy definition because it's "not what I think." *Great,* I thought. *I'm supposed to write something without knowing what I'm writing. That sounds… Messy.* To which my heart quickly responded:

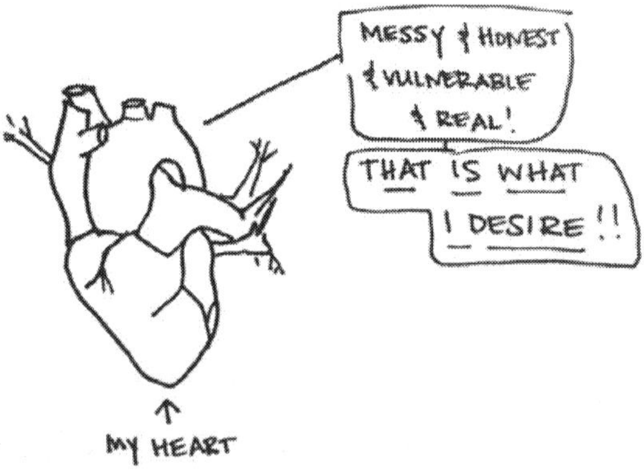

Sigh.

I went upstairs to brush my teeth and prepare for sleep. I felt energy pulsating through my body and I desperately wanted to write, but I still had *no idea what to write.* At that moment, I saw the note that finally solidified what I needed to do. There, in magenta dry erase marker in the middle of my bathroom mirror, was the following:

Write what you really want to say.

The funny thing is, *I don't remember ever having written this note.* This is when everything fell into alignment. I scurried to my office, grabbed my laptop and charger, cantered back to my bedroom, and hopped onto my bed.

I opened a writing program called Scrivener and promptly closed it. I had too many memories of unfinished pieces tied into Scrivener. The same held true with Microsoft Word. As such, I opened a program I had never before used: Notepad.

I began writing. The first sentence of the book? "What I really want to say is…"

In the next four weeks, I wrote the entire book you are now holding. I did so without going back and reading anything I'd written until the book was done. Any time I felt fearful, sad, anxious, or even suicidal, I used the energy of the emotion to continue creating. I pushed the gas pedal down and trusted that somehow the Passion Wagon would continue to follow the unraveling of my knotted insides.

It has been a messy, uncomfortable, unpredictable process. By embracing rather than fighting this, the book pretty much wrote itself. It simply used me as the stenographer.

And here is what it told me to say, in the exact order it told me to say it.

~ * ~

What I really want to say is that I struggled to begin this sentence because I felt committed to whatever words ultimately left my fingers. *Oh no,* I thought. *This first sentence is the hardest one. This is what shapes the entire book.* Something as simple as a sentence, which begins with something as simple as one letter, gets blown up in my mind into this nail-spitting dragon waiting to impale me for any wrong decision. What I have discovered, time and time again, is that there is no wrong decision. This is especially true when it comes to writing. Realistically, I'm either going to write what needs to come out... Or I'm going to write some kind of bullshit, deal with irritability and discomfort and writer's block, and eventually surrender to the words that actually want to come out rather than the ones I think I should say.

What do I think I should say? I think I should spit wisdom. I think I should speak eloquently, without any mistakes. *How will people take me seriously,* I ask myself, *if I misuse a semi-colon or have a run-on sentence?* My usual way of writing is to write a few sentences, read the sentences, make adjustments, reread the few sentences, make adjustments, write another sentence or two, read all sentences, and make more adjustments. The one benefit of this approach is that, by the end of the piece, I will have a nearly finalized draft. The big problem with this perfectionistic and obsessive way of writing is that it rarely results in a finished product. And by rarely I mean that I have roughly 27 stories/movies/books/plays that I have begun only to give up shortly thereafter, promising myself I'd pick up where I left off some other day.

I imagine all of these characters I've created sitting in the last place I left them, anxiously awaiting my fingers on the keyboard or pen to paper. I create these alternate Universes, all of which reflect some inner part of me—something for which I yearn or something I need to heal—and then I leave them under construction. This has resulted in much unfinished business.

Then, when I do get the itch to write, I stress myself out over which is the right idea to work on. And by "right" idea, I normally mean: Which idea will I actually complete that will then, in turn, make me money? Yes. I desire to make a living as a writer. For a long time, my focus was to be a NY Times best-selling author and/or an Academy Award-winner for best written screenplay. I cared about the fame and the fortune and the pretty dresses and, ideally, a private chef and someone who would custom make jeans that prevent my butt from popping out when bending over. Now, the "rightness" is regarding which idea will help the most people. There's really no quantifiable answer to this curiosity, yet I still heavily interrogate my brain gerbils on a regular basis.

I've known since I was a kid that I was put on this earth to write. In fact, I wanted to be the youngest published author ever. Creeping up on completing my thirtieth trip around the sun, I believe I've missed the cut-off date for that.

I have this illusion of permanence that I apply all throughout my life. If I begin a book with a wonky sentence, I get it caught in my mind that the sentence will forever remain. I momentarily forget about the existence of a backspace key or an eraser. *Crumbling up and throwing away a piece of paper? Ludacris! I will instead save the paper and the trouble and NOT WRITE until I have the perfect thing to say.*

Here is what I have realized, and it's a big deal for me to say it and mean it. The perfect or correct thing to write (even though neither of those words apply to much of anything) has already been downloaded into me. That is my belief. As in, the process of writing needn't include a furrowed brow and irritability that I take out on my dog when he brings me a slobbery toy (in an effort to chill me out, no doubt).

It's not something to intensely think about. Rather, writing is all about *doing*. It's about one step after the other, with each word being another step forward.

I put such pressure on myself. I do this all throughout my life. I pressure/bully myself about my body, my mind, and what I accomplish on a daily basis. I also bully my creative ideas. If creative ideas are our brain children, then I'm essentially saying to my kid: "Hey. I don't know if you're good enough (even though I have yet to give you a real chance at growing up and proving yourself), so I'm going to shove you away and birth a new kid."

I'm a hoarder of brain children. When an idea comes to me (or arises from within or however it works), I snag it and get excited about it and then think about all of the people it will help and suddenly get sparked into thinking about the people who won't like it. Before the brain child has even started crawling, I shove it into a dark and crowded folder on my laptop called Jennifer's Writing Projects.

Within that folder is a plethora of other folders with minimal organization. Within the plethora of disorganized folders are even more folders. And, eventually, there are documents. I'll likely never get to some of them. I worry about that. I worry that these beautiful concepts will die with me.

Then there's the opposite end of the extreme, which is when an idea that I've started and set aside suddenly pops into my awareness again in the form of someone else's completed project. *UGH!* I say to myself. *THAT was the right idea. That was the one I should have chosen. Clearly. Because look at all the success this person is experiencing. I really mucked up.*

Or… Maybe the right project is the first one I actually finish. And then the next right project is the next one I finally finish. And if I switch up the order, then that's the right way to do it. Hm.

This results in less of a need to stress out and pick the correct channel for my creative energy. Rather, the process is about utilizing energy to write and to continue writing until I finish something, and then marvel at how things just fall into place and work out when I do this.

When I write, my life flows. Seriously. When I finally buckle down and write what I really want to say rather than what I think people should read or want to read (as if I actually have any idea what everyone else wants), life is easier. This is something I have tested multiple times. During each test, I arrived at the same conclusion: when I write from the heart, everything else works out naturally.

~ * ~

The way the aforementioned bullying manifests into "real" life is that I take a written piece, which was birthed from a place of creative flow, and I begin to plan the rest of it out. "From the heart!" I say, as I silence my heart and ask my brain what to do with sections. "Should they be chapters? Or sections? Or sub-sections? Would it be better to underline or put the headings in bold? I should probably Google what to do about formatting."

Goes to Google

Next, while typing in "What to do about..." that little drop-down pops up to show popular search results and I simply can't *not* read them.

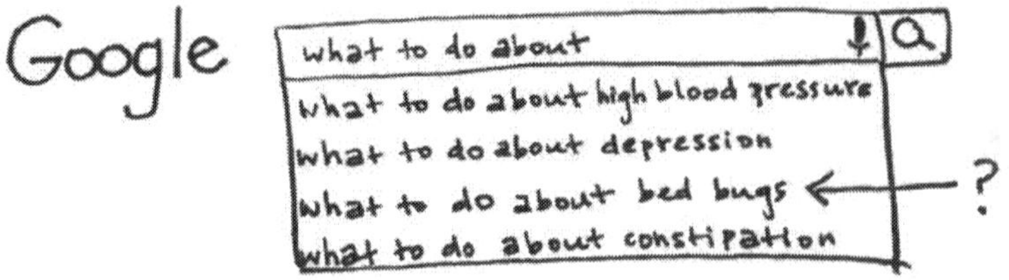

Hm. What DOES one do about bed bugs? I think.

click

scroll

click

scroll

"Oh this is hilarious; I should send this to my friend."

opens new tab

goes to Gmail

sees email from student loan people

click

scroll

curse

click

"PIN? I don't know my freaking PIN. Why does one need a password to log in to student loans anyway? Are there really that many people *jonesin'* to pay other people's debt?"

"Maybe it's saved in my phone."

takes out phone

has 9 text messages from people who somehow only reach out when I'm writing

click

read

respond

This process actively continues as I get sucked into the sticky web of procrastination and self-sabotage. Oftentimes, I waste all of my creative energy on these wild gerbil chases to the point of no longer caring about the heading/sub-heading/chapter issue *or* the writing at all. I've lost the spark. The inspiration has left me. *OH WOE IS ME. THE STRUGGLE IS REAL. I'm going to go lie in bed and contemplate whether that should be "lay in bed" or "lie in bed" but not do anything about it because I am depressed that I am inspiration-less.*

If only I had the right idea. Then the inspiration would stay forever!

Inspiration's got shit to do. Inspiration is like Brad Pitt. If Brad Pitt showed up and was like, "Sup. I'm here to help you cook an extravagant dinner." And I was all, "WOW! Splendid!" And then pulled up Google and typed "how to c..." (as the beginning of "how to cook healthy meal") and then was like, "Huh. How DOES one curve text in Photoshop?"

click

scroll

scroll

click

I don't think Brad Pitt would stick around while I blatantly ignored his existence. At least five other nearly-30-year-old women are interested in hanging with Brad Pitt, and at least that many are interested in hanging with Inspiration. It doesn't even have to be someone famous. If I treated any person the way I treat Inspiration and my creativity, I would be—*I was about to say single with very few friends. Then I realized I am indeed single with very few friends. Then this sound that resembles a firework happened in my head… Except not a nice firework that makes a pretty heart in the sky. This is one of those cheap fireworks that one legally purchases at Kroger.*

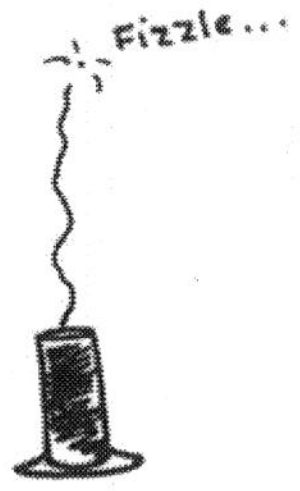

I just had a bit of an epiphany on how I tend to treat everyone and everything in my life. I do so as if they're an inconvenience and are cramping my style. That is, until they leave. Then I forever long for them and feel sad at their abandonment and begin to write poetry with my sad feelings only to instead catch up on Words with Friends with my 92-year-old grandfather.

~ * ~

I am here to write. At this point in my life, I feel the urge more strongly than ever. I feel the urge to write from the heart and—no, who am I fooling? It's the urge to take a spoon to a jar full of almond butter and sleep for days under the guise of preventing another nervous breakdown and taking it easy on myself.

Although, when I nap, I rarely take it easy on myself. When I wake up from said nap, I feel upset that I'm awake and in my current reality.

"You mean it hasn't changed yet?! The book isn't done yet?! GAAAAH! WHY ME. WHY NOW."

flips to other side

frowns heavily

sighs

sighs again

"WHY, GOD?! HELP ME. OKAY? JUST TRUCKING HELP ME."

lies on back

lays on back

*kicks legs like a child who wants a snow cone *now**

Then, once I finish my temper tantrum, I hear a very clear voice in my head that says something along the lines of: *Write.*

It is at this point that I normally toss a stuffed animal or a pillow.

Then, out of guilt, I immediately retrieve aforementioned stuffed animal and/or pillow and apologize profusely.

"I'm sorry, Mr. Pillow (or) Patches Pup. It's not your fault. I'm just really frustrated because I don't know what to do. I feel like there's something I'm *missing*. What am I missing?"

Write, I hear in response. This, in turn, makes me want to toss Mr. Pillow or Patches Pup *again*, but twice in such short succession would undoubtedly be considered stuffed animal abuse—Patches has been nothing but good to me over the decades and Mr. Pillow has always been supportive and neither deserves my anger.

I am currently feeling a little tender about Patches Pup because Floyd, my real-life dog, ate Patches Pup's face one day that I left him [Floyd] out of his crate while I went for a solo walk outside. Upon returning and discovering this traumatic scene out of a horror film, I fell to my knees and screamed, "NNNOOOOOOO!!!!!!"

I'm still healing and Patches is currently in the hands of the most gifted stuffed animal surgeon I know: my mom.

Verizon LTE
10:22
Messages (2)
Michelle
Details
Yesterday 17:54
Patches pups surgery starts at 6 PM, keep good thoughts.
Before picture!
Message

Myself, I have a scruffy bear who has been with me for 60 plus years. I think I will have him cremated with me

Write, huh? Just write. I'm just supposed to sit down and write without a plan or a purpose or an outcome in mind. This sounds freeing. And by freeing, I mean terrifying.

~ * ~

In the spirit of following my heart and my stream of consciousness thought pattern, it appears as though now is the time to switch gears completely and talk about a topic which has taken up much of my brain for nearly all of my existence: suicide. Thankfully I'm not writing this from a place of suicidality. I did start that book, though. I was 23 years old. I wrote one page of it. Here it is:

My name is Jennifer. I am 23 years old. When I finish writing this book, I am going to kill myself.

I imagine your first question is, quite naturally, "Why?" Perhaps you'll respond as most people do; "You're 23, pretty, and have your entire life ahead of you." I agree. I am 23. I'll be 24 in October. I find myself to be pretty. I do have my entire life ahead of me. However, I feel as though I have the right to choose exactly how long that will be.

Before my previous suicide attempts, I quickly jotted down a poorly thought out "suicide letter" that was neither memorable nor appropriate. In hindsight, I realize that it would have left many people feeling guilty or responsible or whatever other human emotion is natural after a friend or family member's purposeful death.

I care about other people. I care about how my suicide will affect other people. I am a writer. It is because of these facts that I have decided to extend my "entire life ahead of me" just long enough to write this book. It has taken me two suicide attempts, one of which had me centimeters from death, to decide to put my two most positive attributes together. I will use my writing abilities and deep care for the people close to me to write an appropriate, memorable, and personalized suicide letter to each person who has greatly affected my life.

I will be writing these to people in chronological order based on the time in my life they most affected me. I will also include actual journal excerpts from my younger writing days to capture how these people truly made me feel during the exact time they were prominent in my life.

Every word that follows is true. Each word and personalized letter is based upon the path that I have been meandering down for the last 23 years, the decisions I've made, and how they've affected me.

I am doing this for three reasons. I am doing this to set my family and friends' minds at ease. I am doing this to cleanse my mind and soul of the positive and negative memories that have been haunting my brain for years. And, most importantly, I am doing this to answer your question. "Why?"

(Present-day note: It pains me to keep the part about people "making me feel" a certain way as I've done much work around taking responsibility for my own feelings.)

Oddly enough, I had that same book idea pop back into my head a few weeks ago. Thankfully, my immense amounts of personal work over the years helped the process to be a little healthier.

23-YEAR-OLD JEN'S THOUGHT PROCESS

I want to kill myself.

But I haven't written a book yet.

It'd be a shame to leave without having written a book.

I'll write a book and then kill myself.

I'll write a book about why I'm killing myself and then kill myself.

This is so romantic and sassy and ballsy.

29.5-YEAR-OLD JEN'S THOUGHT PROCESS

What about that idea of writing a book about killing myself and then killing myself? That was pretty silly and sad and dramatic.

But kind of romantic.

What did I even want to say? I guess I'd have written a really long suicide note of all the people I'd harmed and who'd harmed me.

Why can't I do that now? Write all that stuff out?

Wow, I bet that would feel good.

In fact, I bet if, when suicidal, people began writing out everything we actually felt about life, we'd end up having a spiritual awakening and possibly experience expensive fireworks and all of the sudden know how to fly by the end of it and probably not at all want to die anymore.

Sits down at computer

Starts writing

~ * ~

Right now, in this very moment, I'm really thirsty. I have my water bottle conveniently just out of my reach. I'm afraid that if I move and reach for it, my laptop is going to scurry off of my bed, unlock and open the window, and jump two stories into the recycling bin.

More realistically, I'm afraid I'm going to lose my flow and have this be yet another unfinished project. So I guess this extreme part of me (the one who refuses to move and reach for the water) is planning on writing this entire book in one sitting and avoiding such unnecessary things as drinking and urinating. Yea, that's realistic.

Full disclosure: While finishing that sentence, Floyd began snoring loudly and barking in his sleep. I immediately moved my laptop to grab for my phone so I could film it and send it to my ex-boyfriend.

Move laptop to get a sip of healthy and replenishing water? **No way**. I am *writing*.

Move laptop to film 520th video of dog in order to send to ex-boyfriend at 1:46AM with no attached explanation in the text? …*tempting*.

Thankfully, I didn't take the video. I continued writing. The anxiety I had about moving and grabbing the water still remains.

Maybe I'm successfully writing this book because I'm so thirsty.

Maybe it's the way I'm sitting.

Maybe it's the waning moon.

Maybe drinking water will drown my inspiration.

Okay. I'm doing it. I'm trusting it. I am getting up, drinking water, stretching, praying to whomever/whatever is listening, and then writing more. I am finishing this book. Here I go. To get a sip of water. It's happening.

deep breaths

Okay maybe I'll pray first.

Dear God,

I hope you like that I have started calling you God. I hated that word a lot for a while. I really had a soft spot for Quantum Fred as per Pam Grout's book, E Squared. And, through my hyper-spiritual phase, I liked to say "Spirit" with a whispery voice. So. Yea. I pray to *you* now. Or maybe it's all the same. Um. I wanted to thank you for this stream of consciousness book thing that's suddenly happening. I also would like to thank you for the inspiration to write in Notepad since I felt like Microsoft Word and Scrivener held too many memories of unfinished books.

I'd like to finish this book, please. I'd also like to do things like get sips of water and take mini dance breaks without throwing myself into a nervous breakdown due to fear of losing my place in this book. So. If you could stick with me throughout the duration of this journey, that'd be great.

OH. Also, if you'd like to stay later, that's fine, too. I'm not at all pushing you away.

I know I've only just recently started getting to know you, but I feel like I've known you my whole life.

(I just pressed File and Save so carefully and S L O W L Y so as not to accidentally hit the "Deconstruct" button that my brain created.)

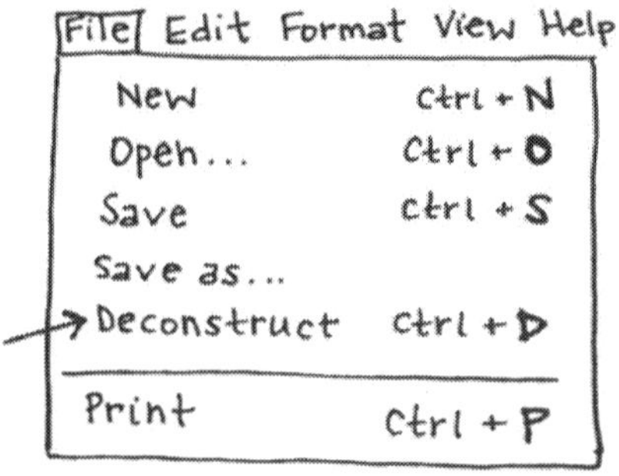

If you could help me utilize the energy of the anxiety I'm currently experiencing, I'd appreciate that. Cool. So. I'm going to take a water+stretch break and then get back to writing. I'm really thirsty. Okay. I'm doing it. It's happening.

Anyway, God. Thanks for your patience. I appreciate all that you do. Although I don't know if you really "do" anything in the way that my human consciousness understands it. I think you're more of an energy. In fact, I think you're everything. Since everything is energy, I think that you are the energy that creates me and Floyd and Patches and my mismatched socks and also the energy in between all of those things. You're pretty expansive.

Thanks for all of this. Keep up the great work. Or. Existence.

Cordially,
Jen

That entire experience was quite reflective of my "OOO SHINY!" approach to life. As soon as something comes up that puts me into a state of vulnerability, I want to quickly divert attention to something else. This something else is normally humor-related.

I brought up suicidality. And then I was like, *Oh shit. This just got heavy really quickly. I was enjoying the witty banter and nonsensicalness so far. Can we not stick with that for 222 pages?*

I imagined someone reading the book, loving it and laughing while eating pita bread and hummus and wearing fuzzy socks, and then arriving at the subject change into seriousness and becoming very angry.

I don't ever want to ruin someone's hummus snack.

But, this is the Year of Authenticity for me. As such, I shall continue following this stream and typing its sweet drops into my loving laptop.

~ * ~

I was six years old the first time I repeatedly bashed my head into a wall to get the emotional pain to stop. I don't know if voices told me to do it or if I decided to do it on my own. This was the age when I began seeing dark figures at night. Sometimes, I'd wake up in a state of paralysis, feeling as if something heavy was pressing down on my body. Other times I'd wake up upside down on my bed, sweating and panting. I had such horrible dreams that my parents created a makeshift bed on the floor next to their mattress. Patches Pup and I slept there regularly. We felt safe there—safe from whatever was in the dark.

I was a chameleon. I learned how to be whatever necessary in order to be "good" and "right" and "just" and "the best." I wanted to be the best daughter, the best friend, the best student, the best kisser, and the best horseback rider.

Since I was so busy being "good" as a kid, I didn't really share emotion. My dad once told me emotions didn't exist. I've since learned that he meant something more so like: "We have emotions, but we are not our emotions." This is quite valid but was not something I understood as a wee little one.

I was depressed from a very young age. The best way I can put it is that I was born with the volume turned up on life. I see and hear and feel and sense things that most people don't. Notice I said "don't" and not "can't." I believe we all have these intuitive abilities; some are simply more attuned to them.

When I was younger, we were rarely able to go to restaurants because of the plethora of overwhelming input. I could hear the conversation taking place via whispers four tables away in between the sharpening of the knife in the kitchen and the screaming child in the bathroom. I could sense if the server was having a bad day or if the people next to us were *really* on good terms or one was secretly upset at the other behind her smiles.

The loudness was more than a sensitivity to sound, though. Even tastes were too much for me sometimes. For years, my loving mother brought cereal to every outing because I refused to eat anything else. While the other family members consumed rich and colorful gourmet meals, I would contently munch away on my bland, neutral, Life cereal.

~ * ~

I was prescribed an anti-depressant for the first time at the age of 13. Zoloft is where it all started. For the next 15 years, I took a variety of other medications and saw many doctors, all in hopes that they could *fix* me. All I really wanted was some help. I wanted to be happy all of the time and I felt that anything less than happy and put-together was a failure and meant I was mentally ill.

That's kind of the message we are fed, no? It's like those commercials that say, "Do you sometimes feel sad without knowing why? Do you occasionally suffer from nightmares? Did that one guy in traffic piss you off?"

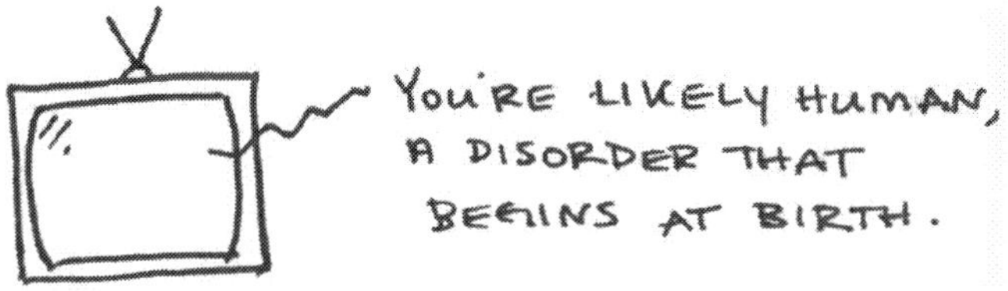
YOU'RE LIKELY HUMAN,
A DISORDER THAT
BEGINS AT BIRTH.

I feel as though we live in a world where we are led to believe that something is (or many things are) wrong with us. Titles, man. For the longest time, that's all I wanted. I wanted titles for why I was feeling the way I felt. I wanted a logical reason for being as miserable as I was.

While continuing onward with my obsessive dedication to be the best, I started working full-time in sales at age seventeen. Since I was in tune with other people's emotions/energies and was able to mold to those around me, sales suited me quite well. This is also where my addictive behavior began to surface.

I proudly did not have sex, drink, or do drugs in high school, mostly because those were wrong and bad and typical, none of which I wanted to be. I wanted to be the special one, the well-behaved one. I desired to be looked at as an escape in comparison to other "normal" people.

I rarely went to parties as a teenager (or thereafter). This is likely because I was rarely invited. *This* is likely because I was that lone sober person attempting to convince people not to drink or do drugs, presenting them with statistics and comments resembling quotes from anti-drug commercials.

I remember being at a party when I was nineteen years old. It was 1AM. I sat at the oval kitchen table in the dinky dining room of my friend's trashed apartment. Rather than venture into the crowd of people and make friends, I chose another companion: payroll. I set my laptop on top the table, sticky with old beer and regret from its countless games of spin-the-bottle, and got started. I don't think payroll was even due the following morning. I believe I was using my action of working hard as a hopeful conversation starter so that I could drop my title of *District Manager at nineteen years old.* I could also tell them all about how I made *so* much money that I was able to move out on my own at age eighteen.

I lifted my eyes from the screen regularly. I watched people funnel beers. I saw others stab beer cans with knives, put their mouths to the hole, tilt their heads back, and pop the top of the can. This caused some physics-related thing to happen where all contents of the container were rapidly released from the can and subsequently consumed. I watched as people went from being articulate to stammering to yelling to grunting to passing out. I did not understand the appeal.

This isn't to say that I wasn't curious about drinking or drugs, as I certainly was, but I remained hyper-aware of consequences. I stayed mostly quiet at these gatherings. That is, until there was an opportunity to interject with knowledge, caretaking, and/or planned bits of humor. When a funneler commented on how much he was burping, I would point out that he'd just ingested a lot of air and give him advice on how to relieve the gassiness. When a partier began not feeling well, I would say something about how she hadn't eaten before drinking and that she was likely dehydrated due to her water:alcohol ratio. I would then find and offer her a form of hydration and a snack.

I remember a couple of instances where I was offered acid and ecstasy. I responded to both with, "No thanks. I don't want to burn holes in my brain."

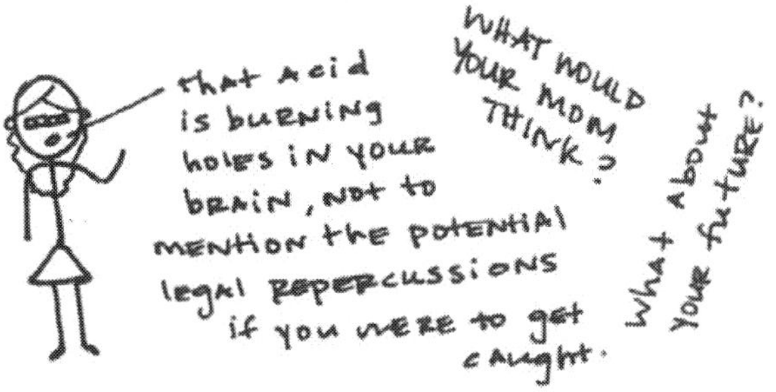

I wasn't purposefully being rude. I was being quite honest about my reasoning. I was sort of a textbook definition of a fun-sponge. Let's be real; people went to parties to escape parental guidelines and ignore rules. I was a walking, breathing parental discretion advisory. It didn't take long for the invites to cease. Eventually, I was only called when the role of designated driver needed to be filled.

Sex scared me because I didn't want to mess up or be bad. Even the thought of kissing was stressful for me. I didn't have my first kiss until my freshman year of high school. Before then, I used to practice on my hand and on Patches Pup (such a good sport, that one). And then, once the kiss happened, it was completely different than I'd ever imagined. It was awful. And slobbery. I cried the whole way home telling my parents how horrible of a kisser I was while sitting in the middle row of seats in their green Suburban, swearing my life was over as I knew it.

~ * ~

I first took action toward suicide when I was fifteen years old. I found a bottle of Advil and told my friend, Icebreakers, that I was going to take all of them. (He taught me how to kiss with gum in my mouth. We chewed Icebreakers gum during this make out session, hence his chosen nickname for this book.)

His response to my suicidality was laughter, followed by: "Why? Do you have a really bad headache?" He continued to make fun of me, which was enough to snap me out of my mindset because of how embarrassed I felt. To this day, I don't know what would have happened with the consumption of that many tablets of Advil.

I thought about killing myself far more frequently than that one time. I felt everything in life so deeply and then felt guilty for feeling those things because:

1. Emotions didn't exist.
2. I didn't want to be like "every other girl." This, in my mind at the time and up until rather recently, equated to "whiny bitch."
3. I didn't know how to express the overwhelming feelings and thoughts I experienced every day.

My parents supported every hobby I ever had. There were plenty of opportunities where I could have positively used this anxious and depressed and angry energy that I harbored. I did gymnastics, I played soccer for a while, I rode horses, I acted in theatre, etc. And yet, I utilized emotion in roughly zero of these. I separated them from my feelings. I went through the motions of these hobbies, but hardly with any attached passion or enjoyment. As a result, my repressed emotions increased in size and severity.

As I aged, I became unhappier.✓ Unconfident.✓ Nervous.✓ Socially awkward.✓ However, my sneaky chameleon genes seemed to successfully fool people into thinking that I was confident and funny and witty. I was even on Homecoming court and prom court and won "Wittiest Senior" in high school. I was always acting… Always playing the role of who I thought people expected Jen to be.

✓ almost every adolescent ever.

I realize now that, since I was so out of touch with my actual emotions and feelings about things and people, I had no idea who I was. I imagine it's somewhat common for a high schooler to not know who she is. Perhaps it's a human thing and has nothing to do with age. Either way, I was ignoring one of the most essential and beautiful parts of my existence: *feeling.*

~ * ~

Without rejection, this book wouldn't exist. Truly. I've written articles and blog entries based on the supposed requirements and expectations of non-fiction writing. I've written about what I think is important or helpful to others. I've acted as put-together and wise as I possibly could. All of those writing attempts and contest submissions were rejected.

After so much rejection, I began slacking on the rules and guidelines and instead writing a little more of what I wanted to say. In the last few months, I have had four articles published. Before then, I had had *zero* articles published. What do these four articles have in common? They're honest and messy and raw. They're Jen.

And you know what? I would not have had the kahunas to write as honestly as I did if I wasn't first rejected for writing the "right" way.

And now, in regards to the book I'm currently writing and you're currently reading (Whoa. Time travel. Weird.), I really am to a point of... "I don't care about rules. I don't care about doing it right. PUCK IT." Seriously. Why wouldn't I write a stream of consciousness book without headings and chapters and page numbers? *Why wouldn't I*? What do I have to lose at this point?

By using this stream of consciousness form of writing, my Inner Critic stands no chance in slowing me down. There are a few terms I'll use throughout this book that I learned from Julia Cameron's book, The Artist's Way. It is a *fabulous* book that all humans should be required to complete before entering adulthood. Or relationships. Or jobs. Just do it. Buy the book. Buy a journal. Buy pens or pencils you like. Do what the woman says. It's magical.

One assignment from The Artist's Way was to draw a picture of my "Inner Censor/Critic" and put an X through it. (The Inner Censor is that voice that tells us we can't and shouldn't do something creative and expansive. It's the one that tells us our dreams are pipe dreams and won't come true. The one that tells us we ought to get a cubicle job that we hate because at least that will bring us stability. It is compiled of the voices of the teachers and parents and non-supporters throughout our lives.) Drawing my Inner Censor as a gooey monster helped me become less afraid of it. I still have this doodle on the wall by my desk, a year and a half later.

Another recommended exercise in The Artist's Way is to hand write three pages every morning. These pages are to be done in a stream of consciousness style, allowing the brain and heart to drain onto the paper. It's a judgment-free zone. These are called Morning Pages and I have done them every day for a year and a half.

Morning Pages were difficult for me at first because I was stuck in this circular logic of attempting perfection. *Whatever I write is the right thing to write but I don't know what to write because I want to be sure it's the right thing to write.* A big part of what I love about stream of consciousness, which I really learned to utilize via the Morning Pages, is that writing is *freeing*. Art is *freeing*. It is not intended to be boxed-in. At least, this is my understanding, which is evolving at this very second. Creativity is a form of powerful, flowing energy. If I snag some of this energy and shove it into a compartment, it will lose its momentum because I've applied separation where there is none.

~ * ~

One day, I decided I wanted to paint. I had done it once or twice while heavily intoxicated off of cheap wine and pretzels at a drink n' paint place in Marietta Square. I enjoyed it. But… I wanted to be a *good* painter. I didn't want the learning curve part of being new; I wanted to fast-forward to being awesome. I wanted to decorate my walls with paintings I'd done. I went to Michael's and bought all of the things needed to be a good painter. I set everything up on the tiny porch of my 575 square foot apartment, I opened the bag of paint brushes, and then—

"Oh no. I don't know which paint brush to use. Are there directions?"

turns package over

"What the duck! Okay. Maybe if I decide what I'm painting first."

stares at blank canvas

Sighs

"Shit. I don't even know what to paint."

Takes shallow, anxiety-filled breaths

"This is stupid. I hate painting."

And I gave up.

This process repeated itself many times. *Many* times.

I eventually read a quote somewhere that said, "What would you do if you didn't have to do it perfectly?" One of my responses was "paint." With a sigh, I again sat down on my back porch with my easel and cheap beginner's canvas, and I said aloud:

"I am going to paint the ugliest painting that ever existed. I'm going to make it so imperfect! *So imperfect*."

Without another thought, I grabbed whichever paint brush wanted to help at that time, named him Mr. Paintbrush, splooged random paints on my little palette and started painting whatever wanted to be on that canvas. Any time I felt anxiety crawl back into my shoulders and chest, I'd remind myself to make the painting ugly.

I don't care what I look like, as long as I'm not BLANK ANYMORE!

The most fascinating thing happened.

I started making really beautiful paintings.

And, hell, even if they do turn out to be ugly, I can say "Job well done, Jen!' and put a checkmark by that task.

In fact, two years later, the walls of my house are decorated with lots of paintings I've imperfectly created and *zero* of them were created with the ideal of perfection.

I didn't realize until this very firework that all I needed to do was apply that same approach to writing.

"What would I write if I didn't have to write it perfectly?"

This. My thoughts and feelings and experiences without filter (with the exception of the occasional misspelling of the F word as respect for my Mama), in the exact order they come to mind and heart.

~ * ~

For the majority of my life, I focused on the negative. I wore a lens that showed me only lack. I frequently pointed out flaws and I lived in a consistently uptight fashion. I worried and complained constantly. Ninja was the opposite. Ninja was my very first love at the tender age of fourteen years old. He was the first person to ever tell me I was beautiful. He helped me out of my comfort zone and introduced me to theatre. We'd play a ninja game where one person would be allotted one karate move and the other would get one chance to dodge. Then, we'd switch turns. With practice, we were able to speed it up and have fast-paced ninja warrior fights.

We dated on and off again for eight years. We rarely lasted longer than a few months because we drove each other mad. Ever seen The Notebook? We were like that couple. If we weren't fighting, we were laughing and kissing. But we were normally fighting. He was the only person I was ever truly myself in front of (until recently). And back then (ages 14-22), myself was *lucking crazy*.

Here's a quick example of said crazy: One time, while driving to our apartment, he told me my mom's chicken was undercooked. As any sane person would do, I slammed on the brakes in the middle of the road and Mortal Kombat-screamed at him to get out of the car. "Ungrateful pig" may have also left my mouth. He called me insane and refused to get out. No matter how bat-shit I acted, he still loved me.

His friends lost patience each time we got back together. (I only know this because I screamed "I KNOW THEY DON'T LIKE ME! JUST TELL ME. TELL ME ALREADY, DAMNIT!" so many times that he finally divulged exactly what they all thought of me.) His response to them? "The grass is green. Water is wet. I love Jen."

Clue for the future - If everyone you know does NOT like your "perfect" someone... pay attention!!!

This still brings tears to my eyes. He chose to see the good in me, no matter how irrational or mean I was.

I remember one of our road trips together, during which our different perspective on life became really clear. He was 22 and I was a year younger, and we had finally withstood each other's differences for a consecutive year of dating. This was quite the feat, seeing as though we had spent the better part of a decade attempting to make it to some sort of milestone without a seemingly inevitable hiatus. We decided to go on a road trip to Florida in celebration. He made the playlist, as he always did, because he didn't trust my taste in music. This lack of trust was solely because he couldn't understand my liking Michael Jackson. He said it removed my reliability as a music critic.

I was the only one with a car and the money to put gas in it, so I drove. We played the Kevin Bacon game and sang out of tune and had passionate discussions about whether or not the word "good" was objective. (I maintain to this day that no, it is not. I believe it is fully opinion-based.) Suddenly, during a climactic point of applying our "good" definition theory to the movie Cabin Fever, the car's air conditioning stopped working. Next, the car overheated. I pulled off of the interstate and into the closest gas station. Ninja opened the hood of the car, gazing at the engine as if he had any clue about the inner workings of a vehicle. Ninja laughed. I didn't.

We spent the next three hours waiting on a tow truck to pick up the car. After the adrenaline of the situation wore off, we realized that we were right smack in the middle of nowhere. On one side of the gas station was a Motel 8. On the other side of the gas station was a *totally separate* Motel 8. Across the street from the gas station was a restaurant that had a giant hand-painted rooster wearing overalls as the sign. There was no name to the restaurant—just a rooster sign.

We went inside the gas station, which *also* lacked a sign and a name, and asked the attendant where we were. He said we were in the middle of two cities.

Upon further interrogation by Ninja, we were informed that the place we were sitting was sort of a forgotten town. It had no name and few inhabitants. The attendant had this blank, wobbly-eyed stare. We asked if we could use a chair while we waited. His response was another blank stare, which we took as a no.

Ninja found a bucket with cigarette butts in it. He turned it over and offered it to me in a chivalrous manner with an accompanying mediocre British accent. We were stranded, sweating, sitting on an upside down cigarette bucket, and awaiting some tow truck man to rescue us from Nowhere, USA. We determined that our situation was well on its way to becoming a horror movie. This stressed me out. Ninja, however, was giggling. He loved spontaneity.

The driver finally arrived. It was dark by this point. Wobble-Eyes came outside and introduced us to him.

"This is Arnold. But we like to call him *fag*." The attendant laughed and Arnold (or "Fag"?) smiled. I didn't find the humor in this, so I figured they were being serious and decided against asking for clarification. They both were missing teeth and there was a smell of stagnant dish water in their immediate vicinity. I mouthed to Ninja, "YOU'RE SITTING NEXT TO HIM." He challenged me to a game of rock paper scissors for the window seat. Ninja won, but he sat next to Arnold by choice.

"Does this taste stale to you?" Arnold asked while presenting a fast food cup of soda to Ninja. I stared as hard as I could at Ninja, zapping warning thoughts into his brain to just say no. My stares did not work. He sipped the soda.

"Yea, man. Definitely stale."

"Oh well. I've got a little something special to add to it anyway." Arnold winked at us both and put the truck in gear.

I was silent for most of the trip, playing mini movies in my head of everything that could potentially go wrong. My counterpart, however, was fully engaged in a conversation with the driver. He asked Arnold questions about his life, his family, and his job. He patted Arnold on the back a few times during stories. There Ninja was, smooshed up next to a sweaty redneck tow truck driver whose nickname was apparently Fag, completely intrigued and smitten. In hindsight, I see that, even at a young age, Ninja had mastered not judging a book by its cover. This is something I've only recently begun understanding.

By the end of our drive, we had learned that Arnold's wife had been in a car accident twenty years prior, which resulted in severe brain damage. Arnold worked two jobs to help pay for her medications and various medical bills. He hadn't seen his daughter in a long time and missed her dearly. He told us of the dead bodies he'd seen while cleaning up car accidents, including one dead lady that he accidentally stepped on. He told us of the ghosts he'd seen. He was a deep, kind, troubled and lonely man—not the smelly creepy redneck who I feared would murder us before we arrived at our destination.

He delivered our car to a car dealership after hours. At no extra charge, he drove us to our hotel. We offered him cash and he wouldn't take it. He said the time with us was priceless to him. Ninja hugged him. I did, too.

It was midnight when we finally walked into the hotel. After checking in, we held hands and walked to the beach, sipping on mini bottles of wine.

"That was quite an adventure," I said.

"That's what life's all about, Babysnakes," he responded. We clinked plastics and put our toes in the water, leaning into one another's arms, fitting together like two corresponding puzzle pieces.

In hindsight, that very much describes my relationship with Ninja. It was an adventure. It was a big, confusing, beautifully intricate puzzle that began as middle school butterflies shared between a sweaty gothic girl and a class clown boy with a bowl cut. All puzzles and adventures must come to an end, and a few years after this adventurous road trip, my decision to kill myself permanently ended ours. Our story is still there, though, as are the lessons within it. The history. The fights. The first times. The wrapping each other's presents in toilet paper and newspaper and aluminum foil. Practicing ninja fights. The '92 Ford Escort Wagon that squirted other cars with windshield wiper fluid. The ant bite kisses outside of the 4Runner. Growling at each other's tummies. Family dinners with chicken and rice. Mountain Dew. Discovering each other's bodies and minds and pushing the limits on both.

Ninja accepted situations and made the best of them. During barren landscapes, he'd search for little signs of life or he'd marvel at a bug. I, on the other hand, focused on how parched I was and how far we had to go until getting to my preferred destination. For years, we shared adventures. And, although we both were experiencing the exact same situations, our perceptions differed entirely. If someone had asked us how our day was going when in the midst of the tow truck situation, for example, our responses likely would have been completely different.

I feel such tenderness in my heart as I write this. It reminds me that, no matter how stormy a day is or how boring a drive is, there is *always something beautiful* eagerly awaiting our attention. And, since what we focus on grows, concentrating on the tiny beauties will invite even more of them into our awareness.

~ * ~

I am really excited to report that life is entirely more magical than I ever believed possible.

I was diagnosed with malignant melanoma at age 22. It was low-grade, but I made a huge deal about it because, well, cancer *is* a big deal. Also, I was amped to get sympathy and love from people. Seriously. I used cancer as a way to get the attention and approval from others that I so desperately craved.

The spot was located on my right lateral breast, which means in between my right boob and armpit. It was removed with two surgeries. Afterward, people were all, "*Our prayers have been answered! Thank God!*" At the time, all I thought was, *Your god had nothing to do with the removal of my cancer. Dr. Surgeon Man and his team at Emory are the reason my cancer is gone. He used sharp tools and cut me open and removed a chunk of skin in the shape of a football and then sewed me up. It's science stuff. Not god stuff. But whatever helps you sleep at night, you lazy praying-person you.*

I thought spiritual woowoo people just didn't get it. I felt that way about happy people overall. I figured they were either hiding how they really felt (which still may remain valid) or were clueless idiots who didn't recognize that every day is a day closer to death. I would get angry and annoyed doing something as simple as going to the bathroom in public. *Look at all of us,* I'd think. *Ants. Little ants marching around. Eating and pooping and washing our hands. What is the lucking point of all of this? This monotony.*

Fast forward to three days ago when I was *beyond thrilled* that I was cooking soup for the first time ever. My prior attempts at soup consisted of taking a whole meal, shoving it in a blender, adding spring water, and pressing PUREE.

This time, I legitimately cooked soup from scratch. I danced around while doing it, recognizing how much of a beautiful blessing it was for me to put my creative energy into something so delicious and healthy for me. Then, before eating, I prayed and thanked whatever/whomever was listening for the opportunity to eat such food. I also took the time to think about the different items in the meal and how many people were involved in getting it from its original source onto my plate. What a miracle in itself! Such a combined effort to deliver a healthy soup on a brisk almost-spring evening in March.

This is the epitome of mindful eating and, admittedly, is not something I do for every meal. A lot of times I instead go on auto-eat mode and scarf an entire meal without realizing I've eaten anything. But, as with everything, it's a process. Each time I mindfully eat and inject my soup with gratitude, I'm helping to retrain my brain toward a healthier, more appreciative way of living.

I know of a variety of experiments where the power of positive thoughts and words have been proven. I've also personally experienced the manifesting power of negative thoughts and words. Having made such a consistent effort to retrain my brain toward an optimistic and trusting outlook, I am thrilled to experience a sensation of joy and excitement around something as seemingly mundane as cooking dinner. There was a time in my life where making lots of money and having lots of nice stuff and having a perfect body wasn't enough to snap me out of my miserable state. Now, here I am, with less money than I've ever had, a little extra weight and jiggle on the ol' thighs and buttocks, and I'm simply happy to be cooking soup.

This is proof to me that the external circumstances have little to do with our true, core happiness. I'd venture to say that happiness is a choice. However, I know that, while in a joyous state, it's hard to imagine anything else existing. This works the same with the opposite extreme of emotion. When I'm sitting in my darkness, I also struggle to recognize the existence of any other state of being.

It is for this reason that I'm choosing to stay present. And, rather than seeking to be happy all of the time, I'm instead seeking to have *acceptance* all of the time, no matter which frame of mind I'm in. *That's* where the magic happens.

~ * ~

A year and a half ago, I had a breakthrough moment regarding cooking. It was with Actor, the one I tend to send Floyd videos to out of nowhere in an effort to say "I STILL EXIST." Prior to this moment, I hated cooking. It stressed me out. Cooking without a recipe still somewhat scares me and results in my calling my big brother (who is a phenomenal chef) and saying:

"CHIPPER. IT'S AN EMERGENCY. PLEASE STOP EVERYTHING YOU'RE DOING."

heavy breathing

"What spices go with salmon?"

Earlier in my life, any type of cooking stressed me out. Because... *What if it wasn't good? What if I cooked something and it sucked? Oh my. That'd be terrible. It'd be game over on life, for sure.*

My primary stressor was the subjective measurements, such as a pinch.

A pinch?

Whose pinch?

My pinch is different than, say, Michael Jordan's pinch.

HOW MANY GRANULES OF SEA SALT DO YOU WANT, RECIPE?! I CAN'T READ YOUR MIND.

This was enough for me to become overwhelmed to a standstill and instead go for a jar of almond butter because of how hard life felt for me in that very moment.

Actor and I were beginning a cooking process together one evening. I felt certain that he was watching and judging me. My breathing became short and my throat started to feel as though it was closing. I was on the verge of a panic attack because of cooking a meal with my significant other. Thankfully, he coaxed the issue out of me.

"Cooking stresses me out," I explained. "There are so many steps happening at once and I get overwhelmed. And this recipe calls for things that I don't have and I don't know what to do about it."

"Take a deep breath, Sweetums," he said, calmly. "There are no rules in the kitchen."

"What?"

"There are no rules in the kitchen!"

"What do you mean, 'no rules'?!" I pointed to the black ink on the printed recipe. *IT'S IN BLACK AND WHITE. IT'S PRINTED. CLEARLY IT IS A RULEBOOK FOR THIS CHICKEN MARSALA.*

"The chicken is still going to be delicious, even without the (insert spice here that I forget because this part of the memory isn't important)."

"It is?" I asked.

"Of course. And if it isn't, we'll add some other spices! And if it sucks, we'll make something else. It's that simple."

"That's not simple. That's stressful. I want a guarantee that it'll be delicious."

"Here." He held out a spoon to me. I did the sideways dog face back at him and slowly reached for the spoon.

"A spoon?"

"I want you to throw it."

"What? The spoon? Why?"

"Because why *not*?! There are no rules! This is *your* kitchen. I want you to see that it won't explode if you take a misstep."

I paused with immense inner resistance to breaking out of my comfort zone in such a bizarre way.

"This is silly."

"Exactly."

I took a few labored breaths. Finally, I threw the spoon at the laminate floor that only kind of resembled hardwood floor. I squealed.

With the help of Actor and a spoon, I had freed myself to let go of this ideal of perfection and instead enjoy the process of cooking. All it took was pushing through resistance with that first rebellious spoon-throw.

Since this is similar to the approach I took with painting and am taking with writing this book, I'd venture to say that nearly every aspect of life would benefit from taking some sort of messy and imperfect action. Just to do it. To get it out of the way.

~ * ~

This afternoon, I felt a little bit of irritability. Most of it, I believe, was regarding the process of writing this book. There are so many unknowns. Also, the way I'm writing this differs so greatly from my normal approach to creative writing that I feel way out of my comfort zone.

Over the last couple of years, I've made a habit of asking myself what I want and what I need. When I asked myself what I needed today, the response was simple: *Dance.*

And I did.

I chose the song "Free" by Rudimental. And, for the first time ever, I danced my whole way through the song without caring what I looked like. In the past, even when completely alone, I still felt as if people were constantly watching and judging me, as if I was on my own version of The Truman Show. My solo dance parties (which didn't exist until about a year ago because I felt so stupid when attempting to free dance that I avoided it altogether) were even shoved into a box. *This is what good dancing looks like,* I'd think, often imagining that whatever crush I currently had was in the room with me. This resulted in putting on a show, in looking for approval, and in becoming scripted during an activity which is all about spontaneity and fluidity.

Today, I effing *let loose*. Whatever my body wanted to do, I listened. I flapped my arms as if they were wings, heavy at first with the weight of the world. I then flapped them more rapidly as my body, via this song, freed itself of energetic attachments to anyone or anything else. I ended up moving the dance session into my backyard, not caring in the slightest if a neighbor saw me. It. Was. Incredible.

I ended my routine on my knees, in silent prayer. And then, ka-PEEWW!!! A firework went off in my mind, accompanied by the following thought: *I will never be the same again.* I said this in relation to how I used to interpret life versus how my awakening is progressing. I am no longer the Jen who hated herself to the point of social and creative paralysis. I have grown out of that old skin.

Yes, I will experience triggers. Yes, I will experience pain. I now have the awareness to handle and process these painful situations rather than stew in them. My hard work over the last two years has paid off in the result of healthier, happier, more stable neural pathways. So, even if I do find myself hiding in bed under the covers, that is no longer my dominant pattern. My dominant pattern has become to push *through* that resistance and self-sabotaging tendency. Therefore, it is only a matter of time before my healthier neural pathways kick in and say *Get up and stretch* or *Go splash water on your face* or *Dance* or *Embrace the laziness for twenty minutes and then start your day.*

The dancing realization started hatching about a week ago. I was in my car after a session with Dr. Dallas, an intuitive psychotherapist who uses rad things like sound chairs to help balance the brain, when I found myself happily dancing inside of Javier (my car) while in rush-hour traffic. I didn't care if people saw me. I didn't care if they judged me. Realistically, their judgment isn't even toward me; it's a judgment of themselves.

Then I thought of playing Call of Duty: Black Ops when I was with Actor and trying to be the cool girl who was good at videogames. Oftentimes, he (or someone else playing) would do funny movements with the videogame character. They'd jump up and say "peekaboo!" and duck again and giggle. Or they'd get caught in a lag that made their videogame character appear to be dancing. Whatever it was, it was enjoyable and fun to watch.

This is how I feel about my true self. I feel as though I (this human consciousness of Jen Butler) am the videogame character. We'll say I'm in Mario since COD is a little too gory and homicidal for how I want this example to be. This human form is the Mario. And my soul/true self is the one with the controls.

When playing Mario, one inevitably gets a mushroom and gets bigger, or a star and feels temporarily invincible. And, unavoidably, one also gets a booboo and loses the big feeling and instead feels small. (Hello, real life!) But, rather than saying "OH NO. Here I am again... a *small* Mario. I'm never going to feel big ever again. Life is so hard!" and sitting still in a decision to do suicide via Goombas, we keep going with the full expectation that more mushrooms and fire flowers await us. If we do stand still, time eventually runs out and then we die. *The end.*

I mean that in as light-hearted of a way as possible. Sometimes it is essential to be still and contemplate the best way to take on the next bad guy or get the giant hidden coin. Sometimes we need to take a breather to build up confidence before taking the next leap. This is why we have a pause button. In "real" life, I'd like to think that this would be meditation or sleep or anything that recharges and refuels our bodies, minds, and spirits.

Similarly, if we come up to an obstacle in Mario, we do so with an awareness that we must overcome this obstacle before progressing onto the next level. *This is how life works.*

Obviously this doesn't 100% apply, because I don't know where Yoshi fits into this analogy, nor do I know how the skeleton turtles come into play.

The concept remains sound, in my humble opinion. My higher self (or true self or whatever fancy word works) is holding the controller while I (conscious human Jen, aka Mario) follow those directions.

When dancing obnoxiously in my car, I could feel the presence of my higher self (or some high-vibrational power) amped at the fact that I'm finally *getting it*. I'm finally understanding that taking myself too seriously is ridiculous and self-sabotaging in nature. I am realizing that I chose to be a human in this time and place. And, most of all, I'm realizing how amazing of an opportunity it is to be human. *Wow,* I now think, *What a fancy human machine I have here. I feed it energy in the form of food and it moves forward and then occasionally emits waste. Fascinating.* That, compared to how the simple act of using the restroom used to infuriate me shows me my progress. And for that, I'm grateful.

~ * ~

The introduction of intoxicants into my body and mind resulted in a toxic love affair that lasted for nearly a decade. It began when I was eighteen years old. This is when I met Bartender, who was five years older than me and worked at a local bar. I was working at a high-end tanning salon in a sales position, which is what first sparked my addictive tendencies. My experience in sales showed me that the harder I worked, the more money and accolades I received. There really was no limit to this, resulting in my regularly choosing 14 hour days with no break. My relationship with work became addictive very quickly. I would meet a goal and the owner would set a new goal. I'd meet *that* goal and, again, the owner would set a higher one. This resulted in a delicious and addicting feeling of accomplishment.

I made more than enough money to live on my own. After a couple months of dating Bartender, I moved out of my parents' house and in with him. The house with my parents was on 35 acres with my horse, Chance, in the backyard, whereas Bartender's apartment was tiny and in a rundown apartment complex. Still, I thought the move was a good idea.

It was in that tiny apartment that Bartender made me my very first drink. It tasted like chocolate coffee and I sipped it while in the shower. I don't remember the exact progression from this first drinking experience, but I do know that, by the age of 22, I was drinking hard liquor on the regular. I did so without a chaser, y'know, because then it'd be less calories. That was another obsession: my weight and, specifically, my thighs. Man, I've said some mean stuff to my thighs over the years. I am shocked and grateful that they have stuck around. I'm still working on repairing that relationship.

I loved the numbness and coinciding confidence that came with alcohol. We (booze and I) became well-acquainted. I worked harder and longer hours, becoming a district manager and corporate trainer by age 19. I left Bartender. Work became my everything. How I felt about myself was dependent upon how well my salon was doing in sales that day or month, or how I measured up to other salespeople throughout the company.

I drank heavily and experienced a revolving door of mental diagnoses and corresponding medications from doctors. They told me I was suffering from depression, anxiety, borderline personality disorder, bipolar disorder, and the like. I lived life with the understanding that something was wrong with me and that, without the "help" of these doctors, I'd be toast. (What does that even mean? Like, where did that saying originate?)

I felt as though I could go to ten different physicians and receive ten different diagnoses. No matter which medications I took, I still hated myself, my life, and nearly everyone in it. After being prescribed a new pill, I'd feel better for a short while. I think this was a placebo effect more than anything. Sure, there's also the possibility of the drug having assisted in the production of necessary neurotransmitters, but it was only a matter of time before my brain adapted to the influence of it. I'd need more and more to get the same effect.

I spent my waking hours strengthening the relationship with my addictions of work, money, alcohol, food, exercise, anxiety pills, and victimhood. I completely avoided anything creative.

Oddly enough, doctors rarely asked questions about my lifestyle. They focused on the apparent chemical imbalance rather than what was *causing* the imbalance.

Few people were aware of my unhealthy way of living. In fact, I'd venture to say that no one knew. I was well-spoken, kind, and professional. The only time I felt out of place was the occasional few hours of sobriety. Chewing an anxiety pill quickly relieved my anxiousness and assisted in my transition back to Put-together Jen. I showed off my smile and accompanying wit, all while my stomach churned with ulcers and undigested emotions. I was rather negative, too, but masked it via self-deprecating humor. Humor has always felt like a safe space for me.

I saved the depth of my depression for my alone time. I spent nights in my apartment with all of the lights off, drinking wine from the bottle, blaring Nine Inch Nails, begging what/whomever was listening to let me leave this stupid yucking life.

I had no idea what to do with emotions. My normal state of being (up until rather recently) was one of numbness. Oftentimes, I'd get to what I now call a "blue screen," which is where I'd become so overwhelmed by life or by unfelt emotions that my system would short out. I'd sit and stare at a wall, feeling unable to take any form of action. Even getting up to go to the bathroom seemed impossible. I'd become an empty shell, waiting to die.

Then, every 3-6 months, I'd hit a bubbling over point where unprocessed emotions demanded to be felt. This normally occurred in my car, where I would push the gas pedal down as far as it would go. I'd play chicken with myself, seeing how fast I could drive before giving up or swerving off of the road. These episodes were accompanied by deep, guttural screams. Other times, I'd drive my car through stop lights just to feel *something*.

I still have times when I experience similar chaotic emotional energy, especially since withdrawing off of anti-depressants. The difference is that I'm learning how to healthily utilize this energy. When I remove judgment around the emotion, I can fuel up the Passion Wagon and write with it or paint with it or awkwardly dance with it. Rather than drive through stop lights, I choose to sing loudly. Rather than punch walls, I choose to go for a jog or fling paint onto a canvas while listening to Rage Against the Machine. The important thing for me to remember is that, although I may not be able to control the ebb and flow of my emotional state, I *do* have the choice of what I do with it.

And today, I choose to write.

~ * ~

I was first introduced to narcotic pain pills via the cancer surgeries. Chewing a hydrocodone and washing it down with a chilled double shot of vodka was a great way not to give a shit. This was a Band-Aid for an ever-growing wound, getting more and more infected as I aged. I was so spiritually sick, but hadn't a clue what that meant.

I regularly reached out to friends, but only to complain. I'd ask them how their day was going only as a leeway into them asking the appropriate responding question of how my day was. I'd proceed to unload on them about how hard it was to be me. I had parents that were still married, who loved me deeply, but whom I barely talked to. I had a nice apartment and a full-time job at a local airport as the Customer Service Manager of an FBO (Fixed Based Operation—essentially a private airport terminal). I had a boyfriend who was a pilot and who had a nice car and took me on trips and bought me nice things. On the surface, everything seemed great. Inside, I felt like I was rotting.

Pilot boyfriend had moved in as my roommate at first. A few heavy nights of drinking together moved the relationship right along. He had just gotten out of a ten-year relationship and explained that he wanted time to be single. If someone said that to me nowadays, I'd be like: "Heck yea, brother. Take a year. Or five. You do you. Best of luck." Back then, though, I interpreted such a statement as a double dog dare. And I *never* said no to a double dog dare.

I remember trying to sell him on the idea of being with me. I was like, "My legs are always shaved,

I clean, I pay for dinners, I put out..." Seriously. He was still unsure. Rightfully so, in hindsight. I was a codependent alcoholic who was giving this dude a sales pitch on why he should be my boyfriend.

I was so disconnected from my inner truth that I thought the only way to keep a partner happy was to go through a to-do list of "how to be a good girlfriend." (I never imagined that the best thing I could do for a partner was to be myself, love myself, be honest, and be a good listener. That tasty bit of knowledge has only been a recent development.)

The day I went in for my first cancer surgery, he decided he wanted to be my boyfriend. (Nothing says "true love" like choosing to be with someone because they might die.) We managed to stay together for another three years after that, both of us pretending to be people we weren't. We were very good to the other on the surface. I did all of the good girlfriend things and he did all of the good boyfriend things, yet we were inauthentic. We were also normally intoxicated.

Honestly, I barely remember anything about him or that relationship. I don't know if it's because of how mucked up I regularly was or how spiritually ungrounded I was, but I can tell you maybe five things about him. One is that he didn't like mayo. The most important aspect was that we lived together for three and a half years and I never—*not once*—found proof of him having pooped. Never a smell. *Never even the scent of air freshener spray.* He never farted in front of me, either. Not. Once.

Clearly, he was a robot.

As such, I attempted to play the role of robot as well. For years I'd use public bathrooms instead of the one bathroom in our house, or I'd nonchalantly walk outside to fart. This was very uncomfortable for me because I am one of the gassiest people I know. My mom once joked that I wouldn't be able to get married because of how bad my gas was. I told her this was a lie. Although, now that I'm nearly thirty and am single, I am beginning to wonder about the validity of her statement.

I tried to be calm, cool, and collected like he was. It was exhausting. Sometimes, though, my inner weirdness would burst out. I remember one night when I was lying on the living room floor with both of my legs through *one* leg of my Santa pajamas. I was repeatedly screaming, "I'M A MERMAID!" while flopping around. During one of my mermaid flails, I got a glimpse of him. There he sat on the sofa, unfazed, staring at his iPad. As such, I stopped playing the role of mermaid-out-of-water. I put my pants on like a "normal" [robot-]person, walked into the kitchen, chewed a pain pill, chugged some vodka, and then chewed a piece of gum to hide the smell and taste of either intoxicant. I spent the rest of the night sitting on the sofa, pretending to be happy, while secretly feeling nothing.

Not surprisingly, I barely wrote anything during our entire relationship, with the exception of the suicide letter book I started at age 23. I put all of my energy into attempting to attain the unattainable ideal of perfection. Art and perfection,

I've found, do not coexist. In fact, one seems to be the antithesis of the other.

~ * ~

The common theme throughout my pre-awakened life was that I attributed all of my issues to external circumstances. I figured I felt the way I did because of whichever guy I was in a relationship with, or because of the strains of my job, or because of any number of outside things. I was known to make abrupt changes, especially in relationships. I used my chameleon ways to morph into what I called Stepford Jen when I was in a partnership. I would quickly learn about the other person's wants and interests and I'd become those. I would tell their types of jokes, watch their types of movies, and eat their types of food.

I loved the feeling of people falling in love with me. I loved when they said I was unlike anyone they'd ever met. As I said earlier, I wanted to be the escape for people. I wanted to be *perfect*. In the process of attempting this unachievable feat, I repeatedly lost what little of myself I did have. I'd close myself off more and more toward whomever I was dating and, once they inevitably began grasping for me or yearning for my affection, I'd become disgusted and leave. Only upon leaving would I explain to them all of the issues I had *with the relationship and with them.*

In my mind, it was never about me. I was certain that I was being treated poorly and that I wasn't being loved the way I needed to be. However, at no point in time was I giving these people the opportunity to love me, or even to learn how. Instead, I pretended to be someone I wasn't. I pretended I had no needs. I kept the house spotless. I dished out sexual favors, even if I wasn't in the mood. So much so, in fact, that I lost touch with what being in/out of the mood felt like. I rarely enjoyed sex, but pretended to. I never stated preferences or what didn't feel good because I was afraid I'd upset the guy. I shaved every day, sometimes twice a day. I kept my body in perfect shape. I swallowed all tears.

I regularly expressed how low maintenance I was. I suppose this was my idea of relationship security. *If I embody everything they want in a mate, then I'll never get rejected.*

I was so dedicated to this act that, after work, I'd oftentimes stop in a parking lot to rest before going home, as if resting in between jobs. I wanted someone to accept me, embrace me, grow with me, and to endure this game of life with me, yet I never gave anyone the chance to do so. I hid. There's not much else that's lonelier than lying in bed next to a person who is in love with someone else. And that's essentially what it was. These men would look into my eyes with such adoration and deep love. I longed for it, but it wasn't for me. It was for who I pretended to be.

Once I eventually lost the energy to maintain the act, I would leave. This normally occurred when the man of choice brought up the topic of marriage. There was *no* way I'd be able to keep up that role for a lifetime. So, I'd suddenly leave. This broke hearts. I mean, shattered them. And the most trucked up part is that I would have gotten myself to such a level of depletion that I simply didn't care. So closed off from my actual emotions, I felt nothing. Grown men would cry, begging for clarification or for another chance. I'd tell them how wrong they were for me. They'd promise change. I'd manipulate (or "jenipulate," as I now call it) them to believe that the demise of the relationship was their fault. In actuality, my falsities and facades were the root causes.

This has only been a recent development in the forefront of my awareness. I have been receiving many slices of humble pie lately, where I am suddenly smashed in the face with a realization of the pain I have caused another. Prior to these moments, such situations lived in the limiting box of "NOT MY FAULT." That box is nearly empty now, thankfully, due to all of the work I've done. It's a hard thing to come to terms with, though; the pain and heartache that I caused others. It is because of this knowledge, though, that I can choose a different path in my present and future relationships. Even today, I deal with anxiety about expressing otherwise simple needs or preferences to a member of the opposite sex. The only way to become comfortable doing so, though, is to simply *do* it. That is the way I choose to transmute the pain from my past: I utilize it toward making a healthier, more authentic future.

It's amazing to me that I have always been such a tender, sensitive, depressed person, desperate for love and care and quite certain that everyone abandoned *me* in life. Since my spontaneous spiritual awakening in March 2014, waves of awareness have come to me about the protagonist of my life: ME. I've been the main character in every painful situation I've been in. Sure, there have been a few where I was legitimately in a state of being a victim, but the large majority of pain I've experienced in my own life was by my own doing.

The wild part is that I had no idea I was doing it. One of the aspects of spiritually and emotionally maturing that I feel the most grateful for is that I now see the power I have in each action. As in, by focusing on being kind to myself and kind to others without a secret agenda (which I still discover from time to time, underneath a few other healing layers), I attract more kindness to my life. By getting in touch with my own wants and needs (and expressing these to people), I no longer deal with such heavy depletion. By consistently being messy and authentic and taking wobbly, vulnerable steps forward, I have finally begun attracting people in my life who *do* love the Real Jen.

The adoration I feel from people is no longer directed toward a façade. This is a reflection of the fact that *I* no longer direct love toward some fake, Barbie Jen. The more I love who I am right now, the more people I will attract who share the same sentiment. The more I accept and support my present self, the more opportunities will find their way to me. The book I'm writing now, for instance, is something I've wanted to write for a long time. However, it wasn't until I embraced who and where I am now (in all my imperfect glory) that the words started to flow.

~ * ~

The depths of my darkness became apparent to me after I found out that I was cancer free. The loving phone calls stopped coming in. The Facebook support. The sympathy. It all ended. During my short dance with cancer, I felt as though I was finally getting a taste of how I wanted life to be: a bunch of people giving me loving attention without expecting anything in return.

I continued to grasp for attention, so much so that I pushed people away. Some stopped talking to me entirely without any explanation. Those slices of humble pie have since been the hardest to swallow. It was much easier to hang out with my mini violinist back then, bitching about how people just couldn't handle my intensity and how no one cared and I was all alone, etc. Realizing that people had stopped talking to me because I was leeching onto them for dear life and then dropping the ball when they asked anything of me was—and still is—deeply humbling. I have made many amends and will continue to do so, quite possibly for the rest of my life.

In March 2009, a few months after the cancer-free diagnosis, I made the decision to kill myself while Robot was on a work trip in the Bahamas. It was something I'd obsessed about for years. I had fantasized about what it would have been like at my funeral, who would have shown up, and how many people would have "felt badly for how much they'd hurt me."

One of my deepest fears was that I was a burden on others. (I still dabble in this fear when depression creeps back up.) I kept myself hidden in a dark corner of my psyche behind [what has since felt like] thousands of masks of how I thought I should be for other people. This ideal changed based on who I was around, so as to maintain my role as the funny, low-maintenance friend, Jen. I was either playing the role of this fake Jen or dwelling in victimhood; there was rarely an in between. I hated who I had become, but I didn't know any other way to be.

This particular night in March, I took out my phone to search for someone to call. I didn't necessarily *want* to kill myself but I knew that I didn't want to live anymore. If there was a switch that allowed me to cease existence, I'd have flipped it. The pain of living, to me, had officially overcome the pain of dying. I called a few people and no one answered. I took this as a sign that it was time to go.

I snagged my hydrocodone and the variety of anxiety pills I'd gathered from the different doctors' prescriptions over the years and I swallowed them. I have told this story so many times over the years and used to over-dramatize stories, so I do not remember the exact number of pills. I know that I chewed some and swallowed the others. My guess is 15-20 hydrocodone and another 10 time-released anxiety pills. I was serious about dying. In fact, after I took the pills (and chased them with milk because I learned from a Nip/Tuck episode that it helped ease the nausea from overdosing. Not sure if that's true, but I was sort of desperate.), I felt relieved. I felt *free*. I wrote my big brother a text, apologizing for not being a better sister. I said I loved him. I wrote a few other texts to friends saying something similar.

Then, I received a text response from Ninja. Prior to this particular suicidal night in March, we hadn't talked in months. I had threatened or at least discussed suicide with him before, but something about the texts I sent him must've felt more serious. Within minutes, there was a knock on my apartment door. I answered. It was Ninja's best friend, Balloon-Popper, and his girlfriend. (In high school on my seventeenth birthday, Balloon-Popper threw a pen at my birthday balloon and popped it. I cried and ran to my car and left. It took me years to forgive him.)

"Did you take pills?" Popper's girlfriend asked.

"Yes," I said, feeling a flutter of hope in my heart that someone had come to my cry.

Next, a police officer walked in. And then another.

"It's only milk," I said, pointing at the red solo cup I was sipping. Even though I was old enough to legally drink alcohol, I suddenly became the nervous goody-two-shoes who didn't want to get in trouble. I was afraid I'd done something illegal. *Isn't this attempted murder?* I thought.

The cops drilled me about how much of what I'd had. The numbing sensation of the pills I'd chewed was well in effect, so I only have small sprinkles of memories over the next 48 hours. I remember being walked into the ambulance. By that time, the anxiety pills were kicking in. I began to slip away.

"I'm sorry for troubling you with this," I slurred to the EMT.

"It's okay," he assured me, "Happens all of the time." This response further solidified my choice for death. *Why would I want to live in such a painful world where so many want to die?* He also told me an interesting statistic, which was that the highest number of suicides occur on Sunday nights. (My guess for this is that people are *that* unhappy about having to go back to work the next day. Isn't that sad?!)

I told him he had pretty eyes.

And then, he was gone. I was gone.

When I regained a slight bit of awareness, I was on a hospital bed, hooked up to all sorts of equipment. I was in my underwear.

"I'm sorry I didn't wear nicer underwear," I attempted to say to the blur who appeared to be a *male nurse. After attempting to kill myself, my first conscious thought was that a nurse may be judging the fact that I chose cotton boy shorts rather than a lacy thong.

My parents were there. My mom since told me that my brother knew something was up by the tone of my text, so he and my parents piled in the car and went to my apartment. Apparently, they went there with the assumption that they were going to find my dead body. My dad looked over the balcony and everything, assuming I'd jumped off. My mom tried to reach Robot. When that failed, she called Ninja. He told her what had happened.

And that's the last time that I or my family heard from Ninja. Over the years, I've written many apologies. No response. He's since gotten married and appears happy (via the Facebook photos I occasionally

* So weird how you almost never see the term "female nurse."

stalk when I want to poke at old scars). I hope he's happy. He deserves it. His wife is pretty, too.

~ * ~

I don't know how my parents found me in the hospital (because we haven't really talked in depth about what happened, though it'll likely be healing to do so), but they did. My mom did tell me that the nurse told her it was a life and death situation. "A hair away from death," she apparently said.

My mom also told me that I kept calling the blurry male nurse Brad Pitt. (Funny. That's the second mention of him in here, and he's not even a celebrity crush.) (Ahem, Will Smith, ahem.)

Time passed. Doctor people stabilized me. The psychiatrist asked me if I still wanted to die (or something like that. I don't remember. I was residually intoxicated for many days.) and I said yes. They shipped me to a behavioral health facility.

My parents came to check me in. I didn't want to be there. I lost my shit. I screamed and fought and told everyone how much I hated them.

I don't remember much of the visit. Once the anger and shock wore off, I actually felt calm. There were no responsibilities aside from eating and sleeping and going to group therapy meetings. Being away from my phone and from people in my life allowed me to be away from all of the different me's I pretended to be. I enjoyed a day or two off from acting.

It didn't take long, though, for that codependency to kick in again. I befriended the nurses and noticed when they were and weren't looking. When they were, I looked as put-together as I could. I offered sympathy and an ear to the other crazies who I figured needed it more than I did. When meeting with the psychiatrist, I said all of the right things. I knew the scripted questions he was going to ask. I'd been through this interview process before.

I was out in five days with a new prescription to more anxiety pills. Stronger ones, I believe.

Cool, I remember thinking, *At least it'll be easier to kill myself with these.*

~ * ~

I pick up litter every day—on walks with Floyd, in the park, in a parking lot, etc. Wherever I go, there is litter. I pick it up and properly dispose of it. Sometimes, I find really cool things. Last week, for instance, Floyd and I visited the trails of Kennesaw Mountain and I found a half-used No.2 pencil. It was one of the old fashioned kinds I used in elementary school. I don't know why, but I felt as though I'd hit a jackpot.

There was another time, when on a beach, that I found a plastic fork and an action figure. I snuggled them together and faced them toward the ocean so they'd have a better view.

For months, an idea of repurposed trash has continued to pop into my head. The thought is to somehow incorporate the [non-nasty] trash that I find into some form of art, allowing it to be rebirthed into a new entity.

While thinking about this potential project, I realized that it applies to this book, in a sense. Although there are many genres of writing that I have included and intend to include, all of the content is from my past. My understandings and my awareness and the progression of my awakening all come from my past. Even when I experience an epiphany in the present moment, by the time I write it down, it's old news. Writing this book in this consistent state of flow allows me to go through the river, pick up whatever old pieces of me that are surfacing, and incorporate them into this new energetic entity of a book. Painful situations, uncomfortable emotions, times of confusion and anger—these are all aspects that I very well may have wanted to dispose of in the past. Now I can embrace them in a new, refreshing, and beneficial way.

For the most part, I only recently began healthily processing emotions. It still isn't in a fluid manner, either. Thus, there have been fragmented bits of myself randomly strewn throughout my inner landscape. And now, as I write, I heal. As I write, I push through fear. As I write, I become more *me*. *This is the energy being put into these pages*. These words. Each individual letter is radiating with this fear-busting energy of being in the flow and trusting in the support of something greater.

~ * ~

I think that words such as "ready" and "complete" and "enough" are silly talk. I mean, sure. One can prepare a meal and have it be *ready* to eat. Then, upon consuming it, that meal will be *completed*. If one's tummy is full, it can be assumed that this person has eaten *enough*. However, in the emotional and spiritual and very human existence of life, I find that these concepts rarely, if ever, apply. Yet, we still find ourselves chasing after these ideals.

I briefly spoke with a friend of mine today who may be given an opportunity for advancement at a place where he works. He expressed that he feels excited about this opportunity and simultaneously terrified, because he doesn't believe he is qualified enough. What is the definition of enough? In response to his concerns, I had this flow of language come out of me that I'd never before considered. I told him that, when learning to swim, one has to be pushed past what is thought possible. If someone stays in the shallow end, never taking the plunge into deeper waters, that person will never know his/her capabilities.

Growth is all about pushing out of comfort zones. Then, once we feel comfortable again, we allow a little more growth. And a little more. And sometimes really big amazing opportunities fall into our laps seemingly out of nowhere. (This especially happens when we are following that inner spark of passion.) When this happens to me, I normally become terrified of *everything that could go wrong,* want to pull the plug on all creative endeavors, hide in my dark closet, and hit a [consenting] pillow with a purple plastic baseball bat. These times of uncertainty, I’ve found, are when it’s most important to take another wobbly step forward, even *before* getting comfortable in the new level of growth. With repeated steps forward, living in a state of consistent growth stops feeling paralyzing and uncomfortable. Instead, it feels freeing and *invigorating.*

One of the excuses I've used to hold myself back from finishing a non-fiction book is that, with my regular quantum leaps of realization and plates of humble pie tossed at my face, I find myself going back and reading what I wrote, say, a few months ago, and wanting to change things about it.

"I had no idea what I was talking about. Look how cute I was... With the over-exertion of my intellect, all sprinkled with ego. I wasn’t as ________ as I am now."

Here's the thing. That's how progress works. And, as a friend once said to me: "Jen. You don't have to stop at one book. You can write many books. Get one out there. Then work on the next." *But, Friend, that makes way too much sense. Also, what if I go back in a year and read the published book and feel all kinds of embarrassed about what I previously wrote?*

The answer, I believe, is something like this: Writing is not only for me. Sure, it helps me express myself and get some of my bouncy energy on paper, and it helps me sort through emotions and thoughts. However, the primary reason I write and share my writing is with the strong intention and hope that it'll resonate with and help others. Maybe that's what art is all about.

~ * ~

Life is much like school. Let's say I'm writing at a seventh grade level of spiritual/emotional awareness right now. Even though I'll have advanced by this time next year, and some of what I have written may then feel obsolete, there are still plenty of folks in Kindergarten through seventh grade that will relate to and ideally benefit from my words. Further, have you ever heard the freaking wisdom that can come from kids? It's impressive.

When hiking with Floyd, a mom and a dad and two young boys walked past us. The parents went first. A few strides behind, the boys carried on a very intense conversation.

BOY 1: Would you rather live in a fixed house or a broken house?

BOY 2: A fixed house.

BOY 1: 20% WRONG.

BOY 2: Why?!

BOY 1: Because in a broken house you get fresh air every day.

Wow. Someone put that on a coffee mug or something.

Sure, it may have been a kindergartner expressing himself from his age of awareness. However, my 29-year-old self was blown away by the amazing perspective of this child.

We all get exactly what we need out of what we read/hear. This is why, if I go back and read a book I already read a year or so prior, I can find brand new things that I won't even remember having initially read.

Another bit of wisdom from this Ghandi-child was something he said when his brother/friend scurried ahead, leaving Wise Child behind.

WISE CHILD: (sighs) There is so much sour in one pill of evil.

That one hit me hard. Here's how it resonated with me: When I get depressed—as in, heavily depressed where I don't see the purpose of life—it overcomes my awareness. It becomes all that I know. In those moments, I become certain that this is how it'll always be and this is how I've always been. Even if I think back on happier times, I assume that I was hiding this pain or avoiding it altogether. There is **so much sour** in that one pill of darkness that it feels impossible to concentrate on anything else.

Do you remember those Warhead candies?

Man, I strongly disliked those Warhead candies.

I remember I'd pop a Warhead into my mouth and be overcome by the sour taste.

Wait—I got ahead of myself there.

First, I'd watch other people put Warheads in their mouths.

They'd make silly faces.

I would judge said silly faces. By all means, I wanted to avoid making said judged silly faces.

I'd take little licks of the candy, pushing against my face's reactions to the discomfort. *Oh, look how cool I am. I don't make sour faces* ***ever.*** *I'm perfect.* Even with the tiny licks, it was overwhelming. Then! I'd see the folks change their faces to one of pure enjoyment and relief. Yet there I'd be, still licking away at the sourness, trying to control the process.

I feel as though life is an ongoing Warhead. There are the overwhelming sour times (and there is so much sour in one pill, am I right?) and, once those times are embraced and/or survived, there's the sweet gooey inside.

Take that home. Chew on it. It's delicious.

WARHEADS
EXTREMELY SOUR
= LIFE
DON'T GIVE UP.
THERE'S SWEETNESS AFTER ALL OF THE SOUR.

By incorporating this mindset (which I began doing the day that child spit wisdom in my direction), I've begun feeling acceptance around my emotions. Even the painful ones. There's this knowingness that this too shall pass. Even when it seems like all that exists is sourness or suicidality or cellulite on my thighs, I remember that vibrant kid and his viewpoint on life. I tell myself that, even though nothing else seems to exist in this very moment, the sourness of this pill will wear off. The sweet gooeyness is on its way to me. Also, in having torn down the shaky foundation of my inner world and begun rebuilding it, I get the privilege of fresh air in my broken house.

The other side of the sour logic, of course, is that once the sweet gooeyness has arrived, it's rather easy for me to go "OH NO THAT MEANS THAT SOUR IS UP NEXT." Thankfully, I've learned that the sourest times are what yield the biggest breakthroughs in awareness and growth. So really, I can chill out and embrace all of it.

~ * ~

Being in physical pain used to be a normal occurrence for me. I dealt with joint pain, lethargy, stomach bloating, itchy skin, numb hands and feet, blurry vision, and headaches. At one point, I visited a rheumatologist. I wish I remembered his name because he was one of the first people to set me on the right path. I'd gotten to a point where the joints in my fingers were locking up. It felt as though they needed oil.

"You have enough symptoms to be diagnosed with Lupus," he told me.

I remember feeling relieved. *Finally. A title for what's wrong with me.*

"However," he continued, "By adding this diagnosis to your record, your life will change. Any emergency room visit or complaint will be attributed to your Lupus."

I mostly didn't care. I wanted my damn diagnosis so I could wave it around as a reason for feeling as sad as I felt.

"There is something else," he said. I perked up, perversely hoping for another title to apply to my misery.

"Okay…" I said, pretending to be worried.

"All of the symptoms you have can be attributed to depression."

He obviously felt the energetic daggers I sent his way.

"I know this may not be what you want to hear," he continued, "but what do you do for joy in your life? And what type of diet do you eat?"

I don't remember how I responded, but I do remember my face getting hot with deep anger. *How dare he take this away from me!*

Eventually, we arrived at a few action items:

1. I needed to stop consuming Diet Coke. For about a year, I drank one or more every day because of the calorie-free aspect. Rheumatologist informed me of the true poisonous nature of aspartame and how that could be contributing to my symptoms.
2. I was to eat healthier and begin exercising.
3. If I wasn't feeling better in one month, I was to go back and see him again. Then *and only then* would he offer me the diagnosis of Lupus.

I never went back. Once I cut aspartame, my joints stopped locking up. A few other symptoms lessened. I started feeling a little better. It would be years before I did an overhaul of my eating plan and lifestyle, but these initial adjustments inspired by Rheumatologist were enough to set me in that direction.

~ * ~

Although I tend to be wishy-washy with some things, such as what to order for dinner or whether or not I want to get married, there are other times when I get a goal in my mind and heart and strive after it with deep certainty and dedication. One example is the book you are holding. It is physical evidence that dreams can and do come true. Although I had little idea how to bring it to fruition, I continued to strive after the goal, knowing in my bones that it would happen. One step after the next, this book came to life.

My stubborn drive and dedication are also what allowed me to buy a horse when I was eleven years old. I decided at the age of two or three that I wanted to buy a pony. I think a lot of girls go through this phase, but my phase never ended. I saved up every penny I found and all birthday money I received. I set up Kool-Aid stands, started a pet-sitting business when I was old enough, and even considered making money by doing portraits of people's Beanie Babies. They weren't realistic portraits *at all,* but I didn't care. All I knew was that I would eventually own a horse, and I was willing to go through any lengths to get there.

By the age of eleven, I had saved up around $4,000. With my parents' help, we bought Chance, a beautiful, flea-bitten gray Quarter Horse. (For non-horse people: Flea-bitten is a color. He hadn't actually been bitten by fleas. It means he was white/gray with black speckles all over his body. Also, although the breed "Quarter Horse" may seem to imply otherwise, he was, in fact, 100% horse.)

I remember when I first met him. He had been shipped in from Kentucky and was in pretty bad shape. A young female rider, Sammy, stood outside of his stall, peering in. The horse's flanks were facing toward us and we were unable to see his face. He was straggly and malnourished, with patches of hair missing and briars in his tail. He looked as though he had experienced a rough life. Sammy tried to get the animal's attention, to no avail. She made a variety of noises, but the horse would not budge.

"He's stupid and ugly," she said. She stomped her boot on the cement.

"He's not stupid or ugly!" I said.

"Well then he's *obviously* deaf."

"Give him a chance," I said to her, surprised at the sudden confidence in my voice. "He's *obviously* had a hard enough life as it is."

"Whatever." She flung her hair and stormed off. I watched as she turned the corner to the arena. I looked back at the animal, who shifted his weight slightly.

"Hi, handsome," I whispered to the horse after a brief silence. He responded to my voice, shifting his weight again and gently nickering. I did a clicking noise with my mouth to get his attention, unsure of his temperament. He turned his head and looked at me with his ears perked forward. His eyes were dark brown, wide, and honest. I cautiously opened the stall door and stood in the doorway. He turned around and faced me. I saw a squiggly scar on his back left leg. I felt such respect and adoration as I thought of all he'd been through to get to that very moment and place in time. He walked up to me and set his muzzle on my shoulder, as if hugging me. His breaths were slow, steady, and warm. I hugged him back, feeling an immediate connection. I was eleven years old and had met the horse of my dreams.

I had always sworn that I'd never get a gray horse. They're nearly impossible to keep clean. I wanted a chestnut (orange) or bay (brown) horse. But, life didn't go according to my plans, which frequently seems to be the case, and I ended up with a white horse with polka dots. I was deeply in love with him to the point that I became color blind and embraced him in all his messiness, as he did for me.

He didn't seem to like being gray, either. Before every horse show, he'd roll in red Georgia clay, mud, and/or manure. There was always some type of stain on him.

Chance and I bonded very quickly. He waited by the gate for me every day. We played tag in the pastures. I would lie next to him while he grazed. He whinnied any time he saw me and I would yell his name in return. I even taught him tricks. Chance and I became the best of friends, and we seemed to fill a preexisting void in each other's lives.

I really believe that Chance is the reason I survived my pre-teen, teenage, and early adult years. I would cry to him about boys and work and money and all the things he didn't *really* care about, but he at least pretended to. He would walk toward me and rest his nose on my shoulder when I cried, or nip at my butt to get a laugh. He always seemed to know exactly what was needed to set my mind at ease. It was as though we were able to communicate without words, connecting on a much deeper level than I'd ever experienced.

We did horse shows, horseback riding lessons, trail rides, and all things horsey. Back in my showing days, my heart wasn't really in it. My heart was more so in the relationship with Chance. His show name was Silent Knight, which fit him perfectly. He was loyal and strong and his love for me consistently prevailed over all darkness I experienced.

He had such an incredible personality. If I was on my phone, he'd bite my butt to get me to stop. If I was sad, he'd wrap his head and neck around me to offer a hug. When I asked him questions, he'd nod his head. (This was really only cool when the appropriate answer was yes, since all he did was nod up and down. Therefore, his performances of this trick were typically staged with me asking the questions.) I never needed a lead line to get him from the pasture; he'd simply follow me.

He was my rock through some of the hardest times of my life. When I was seventeen, my parents began renting a house on 35 acres and Chance lived in the backyard with six other horses. The owner of the property/barn/other horses was kind and generous and we were able to keep Chance there for free, so long as we helped out with shift (feeding the horses, cleaning stalls, etc.). Looking back on this with what I now know and how I now view the world, I think of how amazing of a situation that was. *Wow! My horse in my backyard? The opportunity to hang out with horses in order to work off the cost of monthly board? 35 acres of rolling pastures?! Rent-free living?! Amazing! What an opportunity!*

At that time, though, I was working full-time in sales. I was readily becoming obsessed with work and money and titles. Then, as previously mentioned, I met Bartender and made the executive decision to move into his tiny apartment.

35 acres of rolling green pastures, horse in backyard, no rent... Or tiny smoky apartment with creepy neighbors and a guy I barely knew?

Clearly, option B seemed the most viable one.

I'd work long hours, sometimes staying until 2AM in order to work on reports and schedules. I'd plan to go out and do shift and help with the horses, only to cancel on my mom last minute. So, for these many years of workaholism and growing alcoholism, my mom picked up the slack—as she's always done for me—and took care of the horses. She fed them, scooped their poop, and turned them out into the pastures. Whether it was blazing hot, pouring rain, or freezing cold, she was out there. She's since told me that she did get enjoyment out of it. It was good physical exercise and an opportunity to be around big, lovely horses.

For the next seven years, I didn't spend a lot of time with Chance... or my family. All throughout this time, my mom was still taking care of Chance and the other horses.

Overall, I liked my life less and less. By this time, I was drinking straight vodka or Crown Royal and I drank every day, without fail. It's what I looked forward to. I was so depleted and miserable and I didn't know why. By age 25, I decided that it was likely because I missed horseback riding and missed Chance. I paid to have him moved close to where Robot and I lived, and I began to regularly visit him. It was truly wonderful. It was as if we'd never taken a break from being best friends. We picked right back up where we left off. Any time I was sad or frustrated or suicidal, I'd drive to the barn to hang with Chance in the pasture and feed him carrots.

I had found my relief. Finally.

One morning a few months later, I received a text from the barn manager. She told me there was a lump on the side of Chance's face that concerned her. I drove out that day and looked at it. It was on the left side of his mouth and looked like a large, inflamed bug bite. I figured that maybe he was having an allergic reaction to the grass in this new place. I called the vet out to take a look at it.

When the two vets arrived (a husband and wife team), the husband vet gave Chance a once over. When he went to take his temperature (by shoving a thermometer up Chance's butt), Chance jerked his head in discontentment. Husband Vet, in a serious diagnostic voice, goes, "Welp. I can confirm that he's not gay." I feigned a smile.

They biopsied the spot, which was actually a growth on the inside of Chance's mouth. I stayed with Chance after the procedure, petting his forehead and lying to him that I knew he was going to be fine.

I received a call a few days later with the results. The bump was a tumor, and the tumor was cancerous. Looking back on this now, I realize that I didn't feel anything about the diagnosis. In fact, there's a lot I still need to feel about this tragedy. At the time, I was removed from my true emotions and so accustomed to living in survival mode that I immediately went into Ms. Fix-it mentality. *What are the next steps? Who do I call? What are the options?* That type of thing.

Husband Vet put me in touch with a surgeon with a really weird name at Auburn University. He explained the type of cancer and that it was very aggressive. I needed to get him to the University ASAP.

I began writing a blog called "Give Chance a Chance" and posted it to Facebook. I included a PayPal link for donations. People shared the daily posts and, within a few days, we'd raised over $3,000. It was so moving to see how many people stepped up to help during such a time of need. It was also my first glimpse into the power of words.

I decided to do a photo shoot before taking Chance to Auburn. When I arrived to the barn, Chance had somehow managed to cover his entire body with red Georgia clay. I laughed and took pictures.

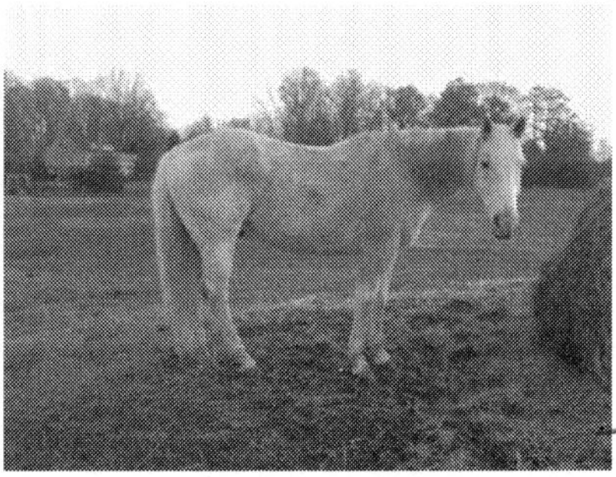

YOUR LIFE MADE A HUGE DIFFERENCE CHANCE!

Dr. Weird Name did an MRI on Chance, discovering that the cancer had infiltrated his left jaw bone. The options were to either do some radiation bead therapy or an extensive surgery where the left side of the jaw would be removed and replaced by a metal one. As tempting as it was to have a bionic horse, either of these options meant extensive stall time and a lot of discomfort for Chance. Also, neither was guaranteed. Dr. Weird Name essentially said they'd be buying us time and that a full recovery was not possible.

After a night of heavy drinking in a hotel room, I made a decision to have Chance euthanized. I don't think I was aware of the decision I was making. I was on autopilot. It's the same decision I'd make now, except I hope I'd allow myself to feel it nowadays. Back then, I didn't even cry. I was far too detached from my feelings.

The next day was my last day with Chance. I gave him his last bath and bought him a copious amounts of treats. I figured a belly ache would be the least of his worries.

He was hyper that day. Feisty. In great spirits. Dr. Weird Name told me that, with how aggressive this cancer was, Chance would soon be visibly in pain. I wanted to let him go before he got into a state of misery. So I did.

After letting him graze and getting lots of last pictures together, I informed Chance's nurse that we were ready for the next (and last) step.

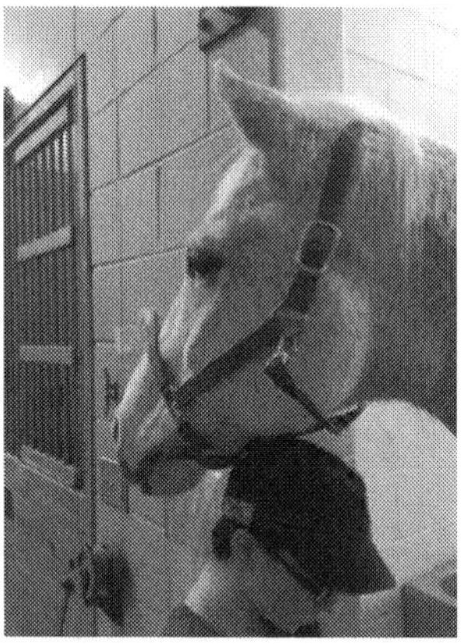

~ * ~

The date was December 29th, 2011. It was a brisk afternoon, and it was set to be Chance's last. The University kept this clay stuff to make a mold of an animal's paw as a token of remembrance. We combined a bunch of the clay in order to make a big enough area to fit Chance's hoof print.

After informing the nurse that we were ready, she and the attractive woman surgeon led us to a grassy patch. They asked if I wanted to be present while they euthanized him. My immediate reaction was to say no, but I ultimately said yes. I couldn't imagine him leaving the world without me by his side. I had to be there for him. Also, with only minutes of his life remaining, I wanted to soak up every bit of his presence while I still could.

I handed the lead line to the nurse and I took a step back. Dr. Attractive Woman injected Chance with what she referred to as a "cocktail" in order to take the edge off. It didn't faze him. He just kept munching grass. She injected him with a second injection. He slowed down, but kept trying to eat. His lips and teeth moved slowly, methodically, robotically.

"He's got a large food drive!" Dr. Attractive said.

High tolerance to cocktails and a large food drive; he took after his mom.

Finally, he stopped eating. I look back now (through ugly tears) and realize that that was his last nibble of grass. It was our last time grazing together. He hung his head low in his drugged state. I walked up to him and knelt in front of his head. I touched my forehead to his, as I'd done so many times throughout our lifetime together. Even though he was drugged, he perked his ears forward toward me. He recognized my presence. I didn't plan what to say to him, but what came out was: "Thank you. I love you. Say hi to Wulfie." (Wulfie was a large chestnut Thoroughbred who also died before his time.)

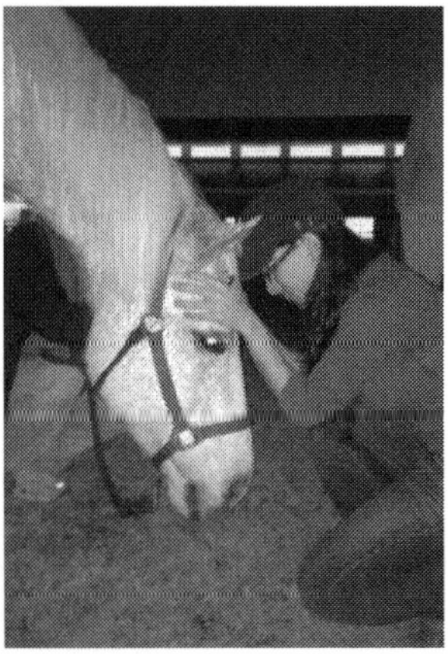

As I view this last picture with Chance, I feel sadness for many reasons. Of course I feel the sadness of missing him. I also feel the still-present grief of having lost him so suddenly. In addition to those, I feel a little yucky because I remember sucking my stomach in for the picture. Rather than be fully present and messy in the moment, I was more so worried about how this last picture would turn out. I've never told anyone that before.

I took a few steps back. Dr. Attractive injected Chance with the anesthesia, which put him into a deep sleep so that he wouldn't feel the pain of his heart stopping. Chance wobbled a bit before his front knees buckled. The nurses and surgeon helped guide him down as he fell onto his right side. One nurse gently petted his forehead while the other ladies prepared the final injection. Dr. Attractive looked at me for final approval. Without thinking, I nodded. And with this nod, a lethal injection was put into my best friend's veins.

He took a few long, labored breaths, and then stopped. I stared at his eye, craving the depth and kindness it held only seconds prior. It was blank and empty. It no longer held the spark of love and sass and wit. His tongue hung from his mouth and rested on the grass. It would no longer lick the salt from my palm or cause that slurping noise when eating grain. My sight shifted to his back left leg with the squiggly scar. I never did find out where that scar came from.

Dr. Attractive, who had been holding a stethoscope to Chance's chest, stood up and walked toward me.

"I can't tell you how proud I am of you for this decision. You did the right thing for Chance, and he was so lucky to have you."

She hugged me. The nurses followed suit. I don't remember responding, or if I even hugged them back. I just kept staring at the scar.

I donated Chance's body to the education program at Auburn University. I explained this to Chance before we put him down. I told him that his sacrifice would likely save a little girl's pony one day.

I don't remember the drive home. I don't remember the few days after that, either. I do remember the phone call I received from Dr. Attractive a week or so later. After the autopsy and pathological reports, they discovered that Chance's cancer had spread down his throat and into his lungs and stomach. She explained that, within a week, he would have choked to death. She again commended my decision.

We had his remaining parts cremated and brought home to me in a custom-made urn (which I was able to afford due to the help of those who donated). It reads "My Silent Knight." This name has more than one meaning now.

The pain I experienced with Chance's death was unlike anything I'd felt before. No amount of alcohol or pills could sufficiently numb it. I felt it permeate through every layer of my being, following the intricacies of my muscles, reaching into the depths of my heart, and remaining anchored in my gut. The simple act of breathing sparked my cells to release the pain to be felt, processed, and released. I had no idea how to healthily feel. I had no idea how to express myself without Chance's unwavering presence, without his big, beautiful neck to wrap my arms around.

Even in his death, Chance helped me grow. The chaotic energy of grief became so intense that I finally felt like I had no other choice but to write. I needed to express myself somehow. I needed this pain out of me. I wrote a story entitled "Horse of a Different Color" and submitted it to a contest at Kennesaw State University. It won first place. I had officially transmuted my painful emotions into something creative and healing for myself and others.

There's this connection between human beings that remains unseen on the surface. No matter how different we are, we all still experience loss, love, pain, and joy. We are connected via the flow of emotional existence. Even though few people who read my story had ever owned a horse, most of them presently or previously had a pet that held a special place in their heart. I remember reading the piece aloud at the award ceremony. By the end, nearly everyone was crying or sniffling. At first, I thought it was because of the sadness of my story. Now, looking back, I see that it was because my story acted as a catalyst for these people to feel *their own* unprocessed sadness or gratitude or love. This, to me, is what art is all about.

~ * ~

After Chance died, I drastically increased my alcohol consumption. More than the grief I felt of his loss, I also began feeling the guilt and shame around having avoided seeing him for so long. There were times when I'd go for over a month without seeing him. I would miss him and think of him every day and deep down it was the one thing I most wanted/needed to do, yet, in the grips of depression and addiction, I avoided him.

I began harnessing all of my energy into a new emotional and physical relief: exercise. I obsessively worked out and counted calories. I did not ingest more than 1100 calories each day. This *included* my alcohol, of which there was plenty. I also exercised every single day, without taking a day off. If I did take a rare accidental day off, I'd feel guilty and as though I'd failed. I'd then work out even harder and longer the next day.

Also, there was no stepping back. If I ran 2 miles one day, I'd force myself to do that or more the next day. So If I did 4 miles on Monday, 3.9 on

Tuesday would have resulted in feelings of depression and anxiety that I was going to gain weight.

When I felt angry, I went for a run. When depressed, I went for a run.

I went for many runs.

My obsessive approach to my body image resulted in having what I considered the perfect body. I loved the way I looked. Much in the way I defined myself based off of my 4.0 GPA or my job title, I felt good about myself *because of* my body. On the outside, it may have appeared as though I was a fit and successful young lady. In actuality, I was starving myself, overworking myself, and poisoning myself through drugs and alcohol. I was slowly killing myself from the inside out.

It was a summer afternoon in 2012. After one particularly stressful day at work, I decided to go for a run until I was no longer angry. I went to Swift Cantrell park and began running... And kept running... For over an hour... Until I felt a shooting pain in the outer part of my right foot. Sunburnt and exhausted, I limped to the car and drove home. The next day, I ran on a treadmill instead of concrete, as I figured it'd be easier on my body. I was barely able to put any weight on the right foot, but I hobbled my way through as many miles as I could stand. At work, I continued to wear 6-inch stilettos, even though my foot was swollen and bruised. I was hardly able to walk in those shoes, but damn it, they made my butt look fabulous.

I eventually found myself at an orthopedic surgeon, who informed me of a stress fracture and a stress reaction, both from over-usage and under-rest. I was fitted with a walking cast boot that wasn't nearly as attractive as the aforementioned 6-inch stilettos. I was to wear it for 6-8 weeks.

No running.

For 6-8 weeks.

My one form of emotional release (or avoidance).

Gone.

I look back with utmost gratitude now, because it took losing these escapes for me to finally come to terms with how miserable I was in the unhealthy relationship dynamic with Robot and, mostly, with myself. Emotionless, I told Robot I wanted to be alone and would be moving home. I did exactly that and, during my short stint at my parents' house, I lost even more weight as I lowered my caloric intake further to compensate for my inability to run. I got down to 111 pounds, which is about 25 pounds less than my body's natural weight. I wore size 00 pants, which I didn't even know existed prior to that time in my life. I remember getting a high feeling every time I saw that number. *I'm so skinny that I'm below normal people sizes.* I remember looking forward to shopping at Abercrombie Kids once I'd lost more weight. I was 25 years old.

The moving home lasted for roughly a month before I moved into a dinky 575 square foot apartment near the university I was attending. It was much easier to have my solo drinking nights with the lights off and Nine Inch Nails blaring while living in my own place.

Since simply *being* with myself was so unbearable, it wasn't long before I was elbows deep into another relationship. I treated relationships with men like a relay race. You know how there's a time of overlap where the runner passing off the baton runs next to the person accepting the baton? Runners = men. Baton = me. I would normally begin putting my feelers out when a relationship seemed to be crumbling. I rarely stayed single for longer than a month.

While reading through this section (after the book was completed and I did my first edit), I asked myself, "What is the purpose of keeping this? I can't think of a lesson to tie into it. I wasn't writing during this time of my life. I was unhealthy and unhappy. How will this be at all beneficial to others?" My answer to myself and other artists is as follows: It is not up to us to decide what is or is not helpful to other people. Our job is to express ourselves authentically and to trust in whatever decides to come out as we create.

As such, the section stays.

~ * ~

I am dealing with a bit of fear around the impending 100-page mark and when I arrive to 150 pages and then to 200... Because, in the past, those have been where I've stopped. I've run out of steam. And by run out of steam I mean that I distracted myself with Google or Facebook or doing laundry that suddenly seemed essential to do.

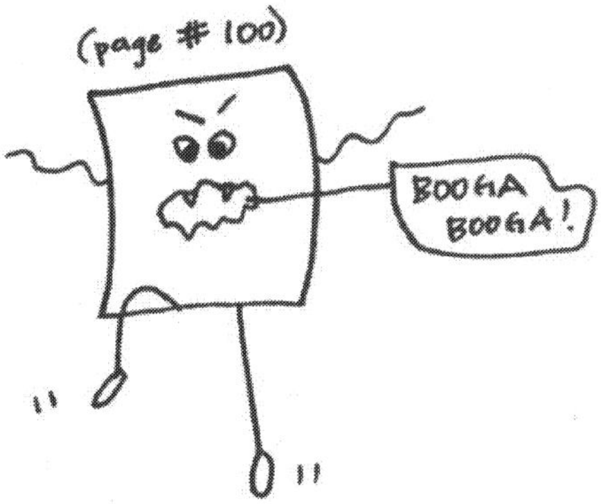

I fully recognize that these occurrences were in the past which, in actuality, does *not* exist. However, the fear around them still does. Alright. What is that fear saying? At the core, what is the limiting belief that is fueling this fear? *Not enough-ness.* That I'm not _________ enough to write a book that resonates with or helps people.

Self-pep talk: activate.

DEAR JEN,

Fear is "False Evidence Appearing Real" and there is no real basis for it at all. You were just talking about how you've grown out of your old skin, right? You've created new yummy neural pathways and have made conscious contact with a higher power of your understanding (or lack of understanding, more accurately) and are plugged into the flow of this book which is 100% YOU. This book is you. It is not you trying to be any certain way aside from authentic, dedicated, and free-flowing.

This is something available to you at all times. This is unique to you. Trust it. Trust the process. Trust that you are supported. And allow yourself to continue living life and occasionally pressing pause to recharge. The flow is omnipresent. You're in it even when you don't realize you're in it. Go. Nap. Meditate. Color. This book will be finished.

But what will I do with it then?!

It will become clear at that time. You're worrying about the next level when you have yet to complete this one. What you learn in this level will prepare you for the next. As such, the best thing you can possibly do is remain present.

LOVE,
JEN

Phew. Okay. Needed a reality check. It's so easy to get caught up in the endless possible outcomes of any certain situation. Realistically, that's just giving myself busy work so as to avoid the potential discomfort of a flow state. Living away from rules and expectations can be really uncomfortable. However, since discomfort is what breeds growth, it's imperative to stick with and push through it.

Oh. Also. I totally am jonesin' for some doodles. I think I've decided at this very moment to add doodles to these pages. Why not? I'll deal with that portion of the level when I get there.

It's amazing to feel this book coming to life as I'm writing it. It's as though I've taken a big ol' hunk of stone and am carving away pieces. The statue of this book is underneath that stone and, as I write, it presents itself to me.

There's a lot that I don't know. In fact, many days I find comfort in saying "I know nothing." At this moment, here's what [I think] I know: I know I'm intended to inspire people with my words and by teaching what I've learned (and am learning) in my journey. I know writing is how it begins. I know *down to my toes* that I'll ultimately speak in front of people with the foundation of this book boosting me up to do so. The *how* is none of my business, really.

My job is to take the next best step. To write the next sentence.

~ * ~

My alcoholism reached a peak during the summer of 2013. I had quit the airport job, quit school, and began working a high pressure sales job that required me to make over 100 phone calls a day to cranky insurance agents. I had started the position in February and quickly became obsessed with being the best. I got to work early, I stayed late, I found and wooed mentors, I wrote follow-up emails for even the most "low-end" clients, and I befriended the nice Asian couple who came at night to clean the facility after everyone [save me] had left the premises. The wife once told me I looked like Natalie Portman and that I was a hard worker. I liked her.

Most seemed to enjoy their jobs, but I felt the life drain from me with each forced phone call. This is likely because of the importance I attached to my sales stats. The work environment was made to be as fun and re-energizing as possible. The break room had a basketball goal, a ping-pong table, and there were a variety of toys sprinkled throughout the office. We were able to wear jeans, flip-flops, and occasionally sweat pants. My favorite part of the job, though, was that we were allowed to have two alcoholic drinks during our lunch break. I very happily (read: desperately) consumed my two daily drinks, telling myself that one double-shot was technically a single drink, so having *two* double-shots was still following rules.

At this point in my life, I was waking up, drinking a swig of vodka on an empty stomach (because it doesn't *really* count as a drink when it's not consumed from a glass, right?), having four drinks during lunch (under the guise of "two"), and then downing either a bottle of wine or most of a 750 mL bottle of cheap vodka at night. I evened out the score by nearly matching that amount in black coffee and energy drinks throughout the day. I had severe pain in my stomach, which turned out to be ulcers and other inflammation due to my lifestyle of addictions, so I took the liberty of nibbling on leftover narcotics I'd saved from my previous surgeries in order to mask the stomach pain. I was constantly numbing myself.

I was oddly proud of the fact that I was a well-functioning alcoholic. I didn't consider it a problem. (Although, I assure you, I had no qualms pointing out the drinking problems of others.) I justified my alcoholism by calling it part of the grieving process of Chance's death. I used his passing as an opportunity to drink without limitations. I did this for years. I remember being in the doctor's office as a nurse looked over my intake forms.

"Oh! This question is per *day,* not per week," the nurse said.

"Which question?" I asked.

"It's how many drinks per day do you have, not per week."

"Okay."

"You put 5-10."

"Yea, that's about right." I responded, unfazed. There was a pause as she tried to decide between moving her rook or taking the easy way out and inching a pawn forward. I skipped ahead a few moves and clarified for her. "So, 5-10 per day is correct. Weekly, we're looking at 35-70."

"Every day?" She asked.

"Every day," I said back, with a cocky smirk. During my many moons as a heavy drinker, I wore my drinking amount as if it was some kind of flare. I felt *cool*—whatever that means. The nurse scribbled some stuff, excused herself, and returned with a second nurse. Nurse One's eyes were struggling to meet mine. Nurse Two's nervousness was apparent through her wrinkled brow and increasing breathing rate. It didn't matter which attack they delivered next, I was ready to counter.

"It says here that you drink—" Nurse Two began.

"—a lot," I interrupted, "5-10 a day. Sometimes more, but that's only when there's something celebrate. Or mourn." I feigned a smile. *Marvel at my wit and self-awareness*!

"It also says that you struggle with depression, anxiety, suicidal thoughts, and ulcers," She continued.

"Yep. And a partridge and a pear tree," I said. The nurses silently shuffled in their clogs and Sketchers, respectively. Finally, Nurse One sat down and paid me in full for the eye contact she'd been holding back.

"A normal amount for someone your size is one drink a day… Maybe two. But drinking upwards of ten drinks a day is doing a lot of damage to yourself. All of the things you're complaining about are common results of…" She hoarded another moment of eye contact for herself.

"Alcoholism?" I inquired, with a beautifully delivered bubbly voice. *I'd better lighten the mood in here.*

"Yes," they both said in unison. They seemed relieved that I recognized their strategy.

"Alright. Dually noted. Thanks for the tip, doc." I began feeling the shift of my tone to trigger-happy and defensive. Both nurses seemed to feel the change. Nurse Two left and Nurse One leaned forward. This time, I was the one avoiding eye contact. I stared at the roll of fat hanging over her scrub pants. Fully surviving [but hardly thriving] on external approval, I spent much of my life judging others based on their weight, hairstyle, clothing choices, and other surface aspects. As I judged her muffin top, the nurse whispered to me.

"We're just trying to help. I'm not trying to overstep my boundaries…"

"Oh, I know you're not *trying* to," I responded, curtly.

She continued scribbling things and took my blood pressure. She told me my numbers, which were something around 115/80.

"Well, at least your blood pressure is good," She said. I presumed a hint of passive aggression within her statement.

"I exercise and eat well," I said. *You should try it,* I thought.

I have since found that, by consistently casting judgment on others and looking down on them, I was living within the dark cave of avoidance. By living in the dark, I didn't have to look at myself. I simply sat at the exit and watched all of the people walking by, quickly scanning their eyebrows, toenails, and physique for what I interpreted as flaws.

You know you're in a dark, depressing cave, right? They might have stopped and asked.

Yes, I would have responded, *I like it in here. It's private. It's quiet. Also, there's only one way in and out, so I don't have to worry about sneak attacks.*

By living in this hidden, defensive manner, I had become the epitome of a person I would hate. I became victimizing, living from a place of denial and blame. I adhered a smile to my face each day and toted a few firecrackers of wit. This, combined with my adaptability, allowed me to gain a handful of friends. Or what I called friends. They seemed to rush to me at first like ants to an over-ripened pineapple. They would devour and marvel at my sweetness until they'd had their fill, or until I exposed what I held inside. This was never my fault, you see. My filter of victimization interpreted every ended friendship as someone abandoning me. *They found out about my true sadness,* I would say, *and they ran.*

My story-telling accounts of these situations must have been entertaining and convincing. I've always been a story teller and I *have* always spoken from a place of truth. However, the longer I lived in my darkness, the more warped my vision became. I was not lying when I told people I had been abandoned; I was telling *my* truth. From where I stood, or, more accurately, from where I cowered, I believed every word I was saying. I assumed the role of the defenseless, overly-kind and caring woman who was repeatedly betrayed. I played this character quite well. I wore her skin like a childhood blanket.

~ * ~

I had excellent numbers at the financial job. The rough part was that I *hated the job.* Being a sensitive person under the guise of being a motorcycle-riding hardass, rejection has always been difficult for me. Thankfully, I have now learned to embrace rejection as a wonderful sign from the Universe which reads "Not this way." Or "Try again later." At the time, though, rejection was debilitating.

I also had social anxiety. This was one of the reasons I drank and nibbled on anxiety and pain pills. They numbed my inner chaos and helped me feel, well, *nothing.* As such, I'd act from this carefree place of [false] confidence, only to become riddled with fear as soon as the substance wore off.

I was drinking at work, sometimes before lunch. I kept mini bottles of vodka in my purse, my car, and sometimes in my cleavage. I smile now because, at the time, this was in *no way* a red flag to me. At no point in time did I consider the possibility of being in the downward spiral of alcoholism. That was so far away from my limited awareness. So far.

Social anxiety, perfectionism, a competitive drive, and fear of rejection all led to me being an *amazing* salesperson who simultaneously *hated* sales. I loved the high I got from closing a sale, but I became increasingly terrified of the "No's."

One of the reasons I excelled at this phone call job was that I followed up with people. I'd actually take the time to send a beautifully written email with a personal note and a twinge of humor. I'd make note of birthdays and anniversaries (normally in my brain or on sticky notes randomly dispersed amongst my desk) and reach out to people accordingly. This translated into fabulous numbers with everything *except* the number of phone calls. I was spending so much time with the other work (and on each phone call) that I made 20-50 less per day than others on my team.

This is what my manager focused on. Rather than commending my numbers, he focused on the fact that I often called 80-90 people rather than the 120-150 others were calling. On this particular day in June 2013, we had a morning meeting where the manager's main focus was on the number of dials we each made. He showed the team my name in red while most other employees were yellow and green. Being a visual person, this was essentially interpreted as a blinking LED sign which read "FAILURE."

So. I decided to call 100 people… Before my lunchbreak at 12.

I downed a few cups of coffee and I told my bladder it needed to sit tight for the next three hours, and I called 100 people. *Tell me I'm good enough, damnit!* I thought toward my manager.

But he didn't. In fact, before leaving to go on my lunch break, I told Manager of my successful morning.

"Do you want me to commend you for actually doing your job?" was his response.

Something happened inside of me when I received his words. My thoughts were along the lines of:

I have done everything perfectly.

I have the best numbers.

I've broken every record and goal set in front of me.

I've read books and studied presentations in preparation for a promotion.

I HAVE DONE EVERYTHING RIGHT.

*AND THIS F*CKER DOESN'T CARE.*

I will NEVER be enough.

Huck him.

Yuck this place.

Zuck this life.

"Funny," I said, "I thought that, as a manager, your job was to help build up and motivate your employees—not openly shame and berate them."

I then slammed a bunch of stuff and left. I also may have flipped him off, though this may be something I created in my head during the many instant replays of the scenario in an effort to feel *cool*er. (Because flipping off a manager is apparently cool in my brain.)

I drove erratically the entire way home. I was at a period of my life where I either felt pain or nothing at all. Those were my two states of existence. I'd oftentimes drive as fast as my car would take me or run red lights. I did this with a twisted hope that I'd swerve off of the road and into a tree or car and die. Or, at the very least, I hoped I'd become injured enough to end up in a hospital and have people feel badly for me and give me the attention I so desperately craved from others (yet refused to give to myself). I obsessively imagined this.

I entered my apartment and immediately visited the freezer to retrieve my solace: Grey Goose. I consumed my "allotted" two [big] shots, but felt no relief. Then, as if my soul wasn't interested in residing inside the toxic environment of my physical self, I exited my body and watched as my human self went to the special spot under the bathroom sink, removed a few bottles with a variety of pills, opened them, and poured a nice collection into my left hand.

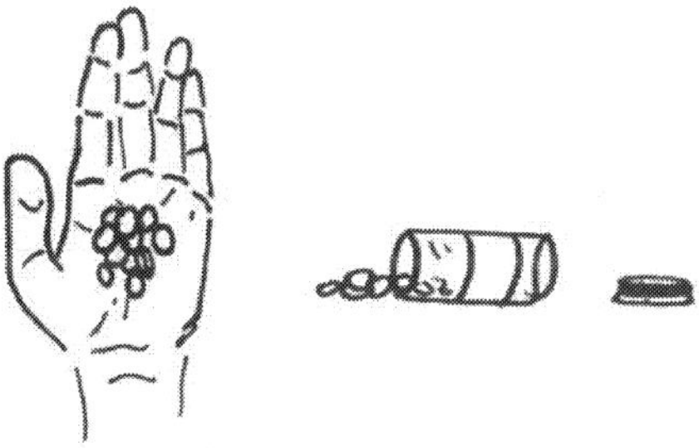

I realized that this human version of me was about to attempt suicide *again.* The difference was that the prior attempt had yielded the knowledge of 30ish pills not being enough to end my life. This time, it would have to be the entirety of all of the bottles of pain and anxiety meds. I also had a bottle of around 60 10mg immediate-release Adderall, tempting me with their deceptively calming blue hue. *If I take all of these pills,* I thought, *my heart will stop or explode, whichever drug reacts first. Then I won't have to go back to work.*

I hated the job so much (and was in such a poor state of mind) that I decided the best option would be to *die* rather than go back to work.

I went into my bathroom and picked up a dry erase marker. I wrote my suicide note. Though I don't remember the exact wordage, I know it said something along the lines of:

It's not the bullied who need the help. It's the bullies. The ones who are seemingly put-together and regularly excelling are those who struggle. The pain runs deeper than can be adequately expressed in words. Why must it come to something like this for a person to be heard? For silent cries to be answered? Find someone who is the helper, the caregiver, the smart one, the fit one. Behind their façade, they hurt deeply.

I called my boyfriend at the time to explain that I was feeling suicidal. His response was,

"But I thought I was doing a better job for you." His interpretation was that I wanted to kill myself because he was a bad boyfriend. To which I responded:

"IT'S NOT ALL ABOUT YOU!!!! FFF*****CCCKKK!!!!!!!!!!" I Mortal Kombat-screamed, walked out of my front door, and threw my phone into the woods.

It felt good to feel anger. My face was hot and my body tingled with life as I went from suppression to full-force expression. I felt insane and like I didn't give a shit about anything and I *loved feeling this way.* Since I was a people-pleaser 99% of the time, the 1% of screaming and driving erratically and flipping people off (if only in my head) felt amazing.

Rather than fluid consciousness, my memory of this day resembles little specks of awareness. Without a transition, I was in the kitchen with a pill bottle in one hand and was once again watching myself pour the pills into my other hand. I was *watching myself* do this but was not consciously directing myself to do so.

Thankfully, the wise portion of my consciousness recognized the familiarity of this scene from three years earlier. I heard a voice. I know it was not mine because it was calm, collected, and soothing.

Something has got to change. The way you're living is not working. Even if you don't take all of these pills but continue to live in the manner you have

been, it will only be a matter of time before you kill yourself. Make a change. Now.

And this is the moment that I realized… ***I need help.***

I was suddenly in the woods, holding my phone. I tried to Google "how not to kill myself," but my Internet had stopped working.

With no other feasible options in my mind, I called 911. At first, the call didn't go through.

I tried again.

Success.

In my most professional and put-together phone voice, I explained to the operator that, although I was well-spoken and seemingly calm, I was truly considering suicide. I told her that I recognized the unhealthy thinking patterns occurring and I felt that I couldn't control them and I needed to be locked up somewhere. At first, it didn't feel like she was taking me seriously. The feeling I got from her was, *You don't SOUND crazy.* Nope. I didn't. I didn't sound or look or act crazy or suicidal or depressed or alcoholic… *Because I was an amazing actress.* I explained to her that, no matter how sane I sounded, I was far from it.

The operator stayed on the phone with me and I felt a wave of compassion from her. This is one of the first times I remember feeling acceptance and love in response to my vulnerability and honesty. I operated under the belief that my inner thoughts and struggles and twisted desires were to be hidden from others. In this moment, sharing my hidden pain and simultaneously asking for help (which was a rarity in itself) yielded acceptance and compassion from a human. It was rather confusing at the time, but it planted a seed for me.

Since I knew where I'd be heading next, I decided to pop a couple of pills and take a shot of vodka in preparation for the road trip. *Might as well take the edge off.*

~ * ~

There was a knock on my door. I answered, calmly. The firemen looked over my shoulder, as if I was hiding the crazy suicidal person inside of the apartment. In a sense, I was. She was well hidden under the disguise of my outer shell.

I was slightly numbed from chewing a couple of hydrocodone and taking a shot of vodka, so I don't remember exactly what was said… But our conversation went something like this:

"Did someone call 911?"

"I did."

"Is someone here suicidal?"

"I am."

There was a pause. This person looked at me in a way that first seemed to say: *Oh, you just want attention.* Then, upon extended eye contact, his eyes seemed to switch to: *Oh wait, you really are in pain.*

"Have you taken any medication?" He asked.

"Yes. Not enough to cause any real damage, though I considered doing so. I know where you'll be taking me: to a hospital and then likely to a psych ward. So I chewed two hydrocodone, swallowed a third, and had two shots of vodka." I walked into the kitchen, grabbed the pill bottles, and handed them to the firemen. I pointed to the bottle of hydrocodone to specify which drug I'd consumed. I knew this would be their next question. "I didn't do so in an effort to kill myself. I just wanted to take the edge off, since this is a somewhat stressful process."

The paramedics showed up. One was a sassy redhead, aptly nicknamed Red.

I sat cross-legged on my living room floor, composed. One paramedic checked my vitals while the other three people stood around me. With their full attention (and my social anxiety relieved due to my substance consumption), I began talking.

"I know I seem fine. Sane. I am well-spoken. I have a high-paying job where I excel. I have a boyfriend. I am skinny and relatively attractive. I have a loving family. I have a 4.0 GPA. To the outside world, I am normal. I am a golden child. I have every reason to be happy. But my inside world is dark and deeply painful. I obsess about death. I've been the good one my whole life, y'know? I pick up litter. I hold doors open for people. I get good grades and I never steal. I've never even had a ticket.* I make an effort to bring joy to the lives of others. I do all of these 'right' and 'just' things. I am a good person. Yet I deeply, deeply wish to die. And few people take me seriously with these claims. Why would they? On paper, everything is great in my life."

(*I had received a ticket but had it dropped after a very well-written letter asking them to do so.)

The firemen and paramedics were silent, still offering their full attention. It felt good to be heard.

Before leaving my apartment, I grabbed a pen and a notebook. I felt excitement about my impending time off so I "could" finally write. (At that time, I felt so confined and controlled by my own high standards that I truly believed I couldn't write. My creative well was dry and I was so numb and exhausted that any attempt at writing turned into staring at a blank page for an hour, writing a sentence, deleting the sentence, writing another sentence, deleting that sentence, and ultimately giving up and drinking vodka. I was a victim to my lifestyle. A victim to myself.)

Once in the ambulance, I was face to face with the beautiful brunette paramedic. I told her she had gorgeous eyes. I smile as I write this because I realize I said a similar compliment to the paramedic in my first ambulance ride, years prior. I normally struggled with holding eye contact. Apparently, when considering suicide and in a state of desperation, I seek the depth of people's eyes. Perhaps, in these two instances, my switching into full-on vulnerability helped me feel more comfortable letting someone *really* see me.

I asked her what she was passionate about. I don't remember her answer, but I do remember using the ambulance ride to be her inspirational speaker. I told her to pursue her passion, no matter what.

I've had this conversation with many random people over the years. Typically, the person tells me they're going to school for something to make them money. I ask what they actually enjoy. Once they tell me, their eyes light up and their energy becomes radiant.

"Did you feel that?" I'll ask. "The difference between talking about going to law school versus talking about being a sports announcer? I saw a spark in your eyes and your entire energy changed. You've got to be a sports announcer. No matter what."

The visual I get is that my presence acts as a lever to switch the train track from going left to going right. It's still their choochoo train and still their track. I simply look within, point them in the direction of their heart's compass, and I walk away. Even when I was in the depths of my sickness, this was a specialty of mine.

I'm realizing more and more each day that writing is the way of following *my* heart's compass. I don't know how to explain it. It's as though, on a quantum level, my soul is traveling and learning and healing and unlocking aspects of myself and bringing my life more into alignment, all while I am physically sitting in my wobbly red chair next to my red Target table, writing what I really want to say.

~ * ~

After the ambulance visit, I ended up in the hospital. I spoke with the resident psychiatrist who decided to send me to a behavioral health facility. I rode in an ambulance there. When I arrived, it was nearly midnight.

I was called into a room with two women (though the term "girls" feels more appropriately matched with how young they appeared) and was asked to strip. I did. I guess they needed to check for weaponry. I felt exposed, but my nerves were too shot from the day to play into self-consciousness.

"Did those hurt?" One girl asked.

"What?" I asked. I hadn't been paying attention.

"Those," she said as she pointed to my nipples, which were pierced at the time.

"Uh..." I became overwhelmed by a wall of embarrassment and confusion. *That's awfully unprofessional,* I thought. I don't remember my answer to her beyond the initial "Uh." The truth is that one of them hurt and the other hurt less due to nerve damage from my surgeries.

Girl One and Girl Two exchanged eye contact and brief conversation about whether or not my nipple piercings should be allowed. To this day, I don't really know how I could have hurt myself or others with nipple barbells.

They let me keep them in. This time around, I was also allowed to keep my journal and pen. In the previous behavioral health facility, I did my writing with a pencil or a crayon. I guess they thought I looked a little too stabby to be entrusted with an ink pen.

After the girls' approval and after answering a questionnaire about just how suicidal I was feeling and how much physical pain I was in (on a scale from 1-5 or 1-10; I don't remember which), I was released into a 24-hour holding area. This is a rather small area where the extra-crazies can be watched before being promoted to a room. The person who decides upon the promotion is the treatment center's psychiatrist. He wouldn't be in until the next morning, so I knew I'd be there for at least another nine hours.

I cozied up in the one available chair. I'm not sure how I got so lucky to get a spot, as the on-watch area was littered with bodies. They were physically alive, but most seemed emotionally and spiritually *long gone.* Some were asleep on the floor. There were small mattresses scattered. One man gently paced while reading an upside-down bible. The rest were asleep, with the exception of the watchful employee. She had a warm smile and offered me black coffee. *Perfect,* I thought, *I'm going to get so much writing done.*

There was a rather wrinkly man asleep on the tiny mattress next to where I was sitting. He snored and smacked. I asked Employee if they had earplugs and was surprised when she responded affirmatively.

Within about sixty seconds, I was holding purple squishy earplugs. Soon after, life was muted.

A nurse came up to me with a small plastic cup of pills. I took an earplug out and shook my hand in a *no thank you* manner. She furrowed her brow and checked her clipboard.

"It says here that you're in physical pain."

"I am," I said.

"And that you have anxiety."

"I do. I mean, look at this place. Not really conducive to *lowering* anxiety, y'know?" I smiled. She did not return the favor.

"This is Aleve for your pain and something for your anxiety."

"No, thank you."

"So you are in pain but don't want anything for it?" I could feel her spiky attitude.

"That is correct. I live with this pain on a daily basis. It helps remind me that I'm alive."

She shook her head, clenched her jaw, scribbled something on the clipboard, spun around, and marched away.

I didn't want to be given more drugs. I knew how to self-medicate and use prescriptions to numb my emotions, but that's not why I called 911. I called so I could *stop* numbing. I wanted someone to talk to me and help me fix whatever was "wrong" with me. I looked forward to conversing with the psychiatrist in the morning. I was confident he'd understand where I was coming from.

I happily sipped on my coffee with no other sound than my own thoughts, which had calmed down since I didn't have to go to work for at least the next few days. Suddenly, Smiley Employee got up to leave. It was shift change. We said our goodbyes. She was replaced with a dark-eyed man who was smacking his gum. He hunched in his seat. His face had deep wrinkles that made him appear permanently pissed off. He said something to me, but I was unable to hear him. I pretended I didn't notice his attempts. He spoke louder. I looked up and removed an earplug with the subtext of *I'm very busy writing a life-changing book, can I help you?*

"Sorry. I couldn't hear you. What did you say?"

"Why you got earplugs in?" His tone felt antagonistic.

"Can I be really honest with you?"

He nodded.

"You're smacking your gum really loudly. I have sensitive hearing." In hindsight, this may not have been the best approach.

"You had them in before I got here."

"You're right; I did. I have incredibly sensitive hearing and there are a *lot* of noises. This helps my anxiety."

"Take them out."

"I'm sorry?"

"Take out the earplugs."

"Um… The woman who was just here actually gave them to me?"

The patient sleeping on the tiny mattress next to me let out a loud whine and exclaimed, "*I* want earplugs!" He rolled over and went back to sleep.

"I don't care who gave them to you," Cranky Employee said. "Take them out."

I complied. I pretended to go back to writing so he'd leave me alone. I felt him staring at me.

"What's in the cup?" He asked after a few brief moments.

"Coffee," I responded, "Black. It'll put hair on your chest!"

"It's past midnight. You can't be drinkin' coffee."

"The woman who was just here gave it to me."

"You won't be able to sleep."

"Actually, I have ADHD. Coffee affects me differently than most. It doesn't affect my sleep."

"Ain't allowed to have coffee here."

"I'm sorry, have I done something to piss you off? The woman who was just here—I don't remember her name, but—"

"—I don't care about who was here. ***I*** am here now. And there ain't no coffee allowed."

"Okay…" I felt paralyzed. In typical rebellious fashion, I sipped the coffee anyway. *What was he gonna' do, lock me up?*

"I. SAID. NO COFFEE!"

I blinked at him.

"Pour it out."

"Seriously?" I asked.

I looked around for a place to dispose of said coffee. He pointed out of the 24-hour area, across the commons room. I didn't look. I stared at him.

"Listen," I said, "I'm sorry for whatever I did to upset you. I'm just sitting here writing, minding my own business. I don't think I'm bothering anybody."

"*Pour out the coffee!*" He exclaimed.

I stood up and walked through the doorway. I had taken one step into the commons area before Cranky stopped me.

"*Hey!* I didn't say you could leave!"

"But you told me to pour out the coffee? And you pointed to the water fountain."

"You pour out the coffee when I *tell* you to pour it out."

"You literally *just* told me, repeatedly, to pour it out."

"You're not allowed to leave this area unless I say so."

"I have no idea what to do right now." I felt high with adrenaline. We stared at each other. He adjusted his posture and took a few drawn-out breaths.

"You can go now."

"Thank you, Master," I may or may not have said. (I was so shocked and angry that life became fuzzy.) I stopped in front of the water fountain. I put the Styrofoam cup to my lips and tipped it back. I chugged the rest of the coffee, something I'd become accustomed to doing first thing in the morning after a long night of heavy drinking. I looked at him from my peripheral view.

"*Hey!*" He exclaimed.

I threw away the cup in a manner that felt most victorious. I walked back toward the 24-hour room.

"May I enter?" I asked in a sweet tone, saturated with sarcasm.

"I told you to pour it out!"

"I did," I said. I sat back down and pretended to write.

~ * ~

Sometime later I was introduced to the staff physician. Grateful to be away from Cranky and finally in the company of someone who cared, I talked to her about my chronic pain. After the tenth or eleventh "Mmhmm" in response, I gathered that she wasn't really listening. Suddenly, her phone rang. She answered it.

"Hello? . . .Hey. . .No, just at work. . .Yea, I'll be off soon."

My jaw actually dropped. A few hours into my psych ward stay and I felt more traumatized than I did prior to calling 911. Physician answered her phone a second time during our discussion. *They can't help me here,* I decided.

This is when I began making the switch to Stepford Jen. I explained to the physician (and anyone else who asked) that I had been working too hard and needed more fun in my life and that the chronic pain was likely a result of my stress. I have since learned how true those words were, but at the time I was only saying them in an effort to evade another diagnosis.

I managed a few hours of sleep on one of the chairs that folded into a mattress. I cuddled under a used blanket left by someone who'd been promoted to another room. I had a window seat, which helped me feel less claustrophobic in the room of fellow crazies.

The next morning, we were all called to breakfast. The food was delicious and severely unhealthy. Pancakes. French toast. Biscuits. (All of which, I now know, cause a rapid spike in blood sugar and serotonin, resulting in a temporary feel-good sensation and an eventual emotional crash.) Over breakfast, we had to fill out another sheet, quantifying our level of physical and emotional pain. I believe we did this somewhere around three times a day, though I don't actually remember. This was the last one where I answered truthfully. I scored high on my suicidality and honestly expressed the twisted thoughts I was experiencing.

The conversation with other patients consisted of basic introductions. *What's your name? Why are you in here?*

"Most people think throwing themselves out of a window or jumping off a bridge is the most surefire way to go," the girl with the shaved head explained.

"Is it not?" Someone else asked.

"No. It's a common mistake. Few people are heavy enough for that to result in death. Normally it severely injures people, but they stay alive."

"Is it pills?" The same Someone Else asked.

"No way," Shaved Head said. "It's actually really difficult to kill yourself with pills."

I nodded.

"So what's the best way to do it?" Another person asked.

"Well," Shaved Head leaned in closer, "You know those underground trains?"

Nods of affirmation.

"You gotta' throw yourself in front of one of those. Wham splat. It's just a matter of doing it without someone stopping you first."

The conversation continued as each patient discussed the way they intended to try and kill themselves next go around. Their tones seemed hopeful, similar to what one may hear from a high schooler discussing her dream college.

I was stuck in the 24-hour room for longer than anticipated. The psychiatrist came in at 8 or 9 in the morning and left in the afternoon. My surrounding inhabitants began changing as some were promoted and other newbies were introduced. There was one woman who spoke aloud in third person as if she was writing a novel about the character *of* herself. I spent about an hour listening to her, desperately wanting to write a play with her as a character.

Psychiatrist eventually came back to the facility. I arrived as Well-spoken, Put-together Jen. My batteries were too low to keep the act going for long, but I figured I could survive an interview.

The questions he asked were scripted, dry, and familiar. I had been asked this same lineup of questions when previously diagnosed with bipolar disorder at age twenty. I answered in the most balanced way possible. By the end of the shortened session, we arrived at the conclusion that I had experienced a nervous breakdown due to overwork. He agreed that he'd order some vitamins for me to take in the morning, as I was hell-bent on not taking medication. I had been taking Adderall for a few months, but I wanted a weekend away from normalcy. I wanted a vacation from Jen.

~ * ~

During visiting hours on Saturday, my dad came to visit. I had given no one else my ID number except for my dad. I told him I didn't want any visitors, even though I desperately did. I simply wanted people to understand what I was feeling and experiencing without my having to explain anything to them. Thus, I decided to isolate as much as possible. Stubborn as my dad is, he came anyway. I felt a spark of excitement in my tummy when the nurse called my name for visitation.

I walked into the room with the chairs and sat in a plastic, burnt orange one. I felt nervous to see my dad. My façade quivered. He came into the room with his usual smile. He kissed my head and sat next to me.

"This place is nicer than the last," he said with a twinkle in his eye.

I shrugged.

"So, what do you want to do?"

"I want to be happy."

"What makes you happy?"

"I don't know," I responded, motioning toward my surroundings.

"How about this," He rephrased, "Where do you see yourself in five years? In a dream world."

"In dream world? I'm a NY Times Best-selling writer."

"Perfect. What do you want to write?"

"I don't *know*, Dad. I have no idea what to write."

"Then write about it."

"What?"

"Write about it. You could call the book... Writer's Block."

We agreed that I was here to write and that, in order to be a writer, I simply had to, y'know, write stuff. Fancy concept there.

He asked if the finance job made me happy. I told him it didn't. I explained that I was there so I could make money to finance my writing career. His eyes pointed out the flaws in this logic. I had been operating under this belief for nearly a decade and had yet to save enough money to finance my writing career.

We agreed I'd quit the job and go back to school. He told me to write first, and that the rest would follow. A brilliant man, that one.

~ * ~

As part of the agreement of my being released from the behavioral health facility, I had to do a certain amount of therapy sessions. The first therapist I went to had a lazy eye and wore Velcro shoes. We didn't get along well. This is likely because I was completely closed off, judgmental, and avoidant. I remember thinking, *What do YOU know about the difficulties of life? You wear Velcro shoes.*

Finding a therapist is an awful lot like dating.

The therapist I ended up choosing was a strikingly beautiful and well-dressed woman in her late fifties. She specialized in eating disorders and addiction, which was a pretty okay fit for where I was. I was still heavily drinking and popping pills, and I regularly had my way with peanut butter and/or cereal. I'm talking... An entire box of cereal. In one sitting. And then peanut butter. And then vodka.

She recommended two books to me: Diet Rehab and Potatoes, Not Prozac. I chose to read Diet Rehab first for two reasons:

1. The full title is "Diet Rehab: 28 Days to Finally Stop Craving the Foods That Make You Fat," which appealed to my body image obsession.
2. The author, Dr. Mike Dow, is attractive and presumably unmarried due to the lack of wedding ring on his cover picture. Motivation.

In this book, I learned about two main neurotransmitters in the brain, how they affected me emotionally/physically, and which foods affected their production. The book primarily focuses on serotonin and dopamine. Dr. Mike Dow shares the brilliant approach of *adding before taking away.* As in, rather than me suddenly removing my daily dosage of nut butter and thereby throwing off my brain (which is accustomed to eating that food every day and retrieving the subsequent neurotransmitters), his recommendation is that we stick with our daily diet exactly how it is and simply *add more good stuff.* Add more greens. Add some organic tea. Add a daily walk. All of these feed the brain its tasty neurotransmitters in a healthy and sustainable way. Then, apparently, cravings dissipate.

What I experienced as a result of this approach is exactly what Dr. Dow references in the book: I simply stopped craving "bad" foods and alcohol. In time, it's as though I rebuilt trust with my inner ecosystem. My brain and body knew I'd feed them regular, healthy meals, in addition to regular, healthy activities. In time, there was no longer the desperate feeling of intense cravings. Over the period of a handful of months, the physical desire to compulsively overeat and overdrink began to dissolve, seemingly on its own.

Before I agreed to read the book, I went through a bout of depression and suicidality that was absolutely out of control. I listened to Therapist's recommendation to begin journaling, which I hadn't

one addiction to another to another to another

done since high school. I started doing it specifically when I was triggered into my obsession with self-harm and death. I also made a list of very easy things to do *instead* of kill myself. You know, healthy things. The key was for these to be very easily attainable. My list looked something like this:

-drink a glass of water
-floss
-make tea

I imagine "go for a walk" was on there, too. But, if you've ever dealt with depression, you know how freaking impossible a simple walk feels when in the midst of such darkness. There's so much sour in that pill. So. Much. Sour.

Through journaling, I was able to discover something that marked the beginning of my healing journey: I learned how long my bouts of suicidality actually lasted. As soon as I felt triggered, I'd write down the time and what it was that triggered me. Sometimes, writing it down was enough to arrest the harmful ideations. Other times, I'd do one of my to-do list items. The rest of the time, I'd stare at the clock until I felt confident enough that I wouldn't try to die, and then I'd take note of how long the entire process lasted. Normally, the really intense ideations (true considerations) would last for 5-15 minutes. The longest I dealt with was 30 minutes. These were *substantially* shorter than I'd anticipated. Due to the overwhelming sourness of each pill of suicidality, I normally found myself believing that I'd always been there or, at the very least, would be there from that point onward. It felt all-encompassing. By taking note of these episodes, I was able to view my situation more objectively... Almost like a research project.

It's amazing to look back and see the positive impact writing has had on my life. During this particular phase of suicidality, writing empowered me. It helped me begin grasping reality and feeling a sense of hope. There was no judgment from Writing. No games. It was always available to me and, each time I utilized it, I felt a teensy bit better… A teensy bit *less* like dying.

~ * ~

I can honestly say that floss saved my life. From my list of "healthy distractions," my go-to was flossing. This was mostly because it required the least amount of effort. I was to that point of depression where I had to sell myself on the idea of walking twenty feet to the restroom to go pee, so exerting any extra effort seemed like quite a feat.

Even normal flossing was too much work for me. Plus, I didn't like the way my hands smelled afterward. I discovered these fabulous little green and minty floss+pick combos at Walgreen's. I think they were intended to keep on one's person for quick usage after a meal. I stocked up on these and kept them in mini piles throughout my apartment.

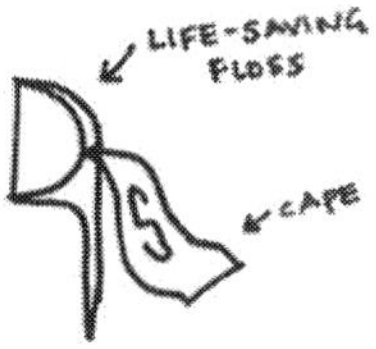

Through journaling, I discovered that my normal triggers were conversations with certain people in my life. I've recently discovered, years later, that a large reason their presence triggered me was because of how much they reminded me *of* myself and certain aspects I was avoiding. Here is what the chain of events looked like following a trigger:

1. Experience sinking sensation throughout body, accompanied by a feeling of the blood rapidly leaving my face.
2. Wonder why no one else understands me and why everyone is so mean and demanding.
3. Think about vodka.
4. Feel abandoned and sorry for myself.
5. Think about fatty and starchy foods.
6. Become certain that life will always be this hard and wonder, *is it really worth it?*
7. Convince myself that it'd be better to drink booze or eat lots of food than to kill myself.
8. Do the caloric math between the alcohol and the food.

9. Choose alcohol because the immediate benefits are greater and the calories are fewer.
10. Feel an immediate and short-lived sense of relief upon taking swig from vodka bottle.
11. Drink another shot.
12. Decide that I deserve to eat the food, too, and ignore all physical signs that my body is not at all hungry.
13. Take spoon to a jar of nut butter.
14. Once halfway through nut butter jar, experience a brief sense of calmness.
15. Do math in head about how many calories were just consumed.
16. Experience guilt and shame for giving into my compulsive behaviors, *yet again.*
17. Upon the return of the emotional pain, feel intense anger toward my parents for ever creating me, deciding they made me for their own selfish reasons.
18. Swear to never have children because I'm that selfless of a person that I'd never wish this hell of life on anyone else.
19. Grab dry erase marker and write angry suicide note on the bathroom mirror.
20. Feel intense onset of physical pain along with the emotional pain.
21. Crawl on the bathroom or kitchen floor.
22. Wonder what the ruck the point of human life is.
23. Crawl toward the front door and beg for someone to come through and rescue me.
24. Realize I'm alone and abandoned in this mess of a life.
25. Cry.
26. Scream profanity at top of lungs while punching cabinetry.
27. Punch self in head repeatedly.
28. Enjoy calmness that comes with the brain's release of oxytocin with the onset of physical pain.
29. Take a breath and wipe tears.
30. Have a congratulatory shot of vodka or glass of wine and crawl into bed, no matter the time of day.

There was a period of time where I'd stop after my first shot in #10. That was enough to curb my emotional freefall. One that stopped working, I added #11. And when *that* wasn't enough, I took it to #14 with the nut butter (or Cinnamon Toast Crunch or Oreos). The booze+bingeing combination prevented me from committing suicide for *years*. But, as with any addiction, it got to the point where those steps no longer brought me relief. That's when I started physically hurting myself.

I thought about slicing up my skin like I'd heard of other people doing, but I never actually considered it. First of all, I didn't want scars on my skin. This was mostly because of the vanity aspect, but I also didn't want people to know what I was like behind closed doors. Although I *did* complain to and seek love from my friends, I preferred that no one knew exactly how dark my inner life was. I only shared bits and pieces with friends, certain they couldn't (or wouldn't) handle *all* of me. Secondly, if I cut deeply enough to kill myself, I'd make a huge mess. I felt preemptive guilt for the EMT who would find me *and* for the cleaning crew that would have to clean up the mess *and* for the person who would inhabit the apartment next. Hell, I'm grateful for my twisted forms of justification. That's part of what kept me alive.

Once I started journaling and writing down my triggers, it gave me enough forward momentum to feel like I could accomplish one of the healthy distractions. *For experiment's sake,* I thought. The moment I was triggered, I would grab for my journal or a floss+pick, whichever was closest. The first time I chose the healthy distraction, it did nothing more than give me something to do for approximately 60 seconds. Afterward, I crawled back into bed and felt angry that *it didn't work, just like nothing else works.*

I didn't stop after the first time, though. I recognized that my usual thirtyish steps following a trigger were *not* the healthiest route, and I really became desperately attached to the hope that there was more to life than being miserable, lonely, and suicidal. As such, I continued flossing each time I considered killing myself.

A few days into this activity, I not only flossed after being triggered, but I also felt enough inertia to brush my teeth and wash my face.

The next day, I felt motivated enough to shower, shave my legs, and get dressed in something aside from ratty pajamas.

By week two, I found myself cleaning my bathroom after my trigger-induced flossing.

Three weeks after I began this seemingly pointless effort, I went for a walk outside. I stared at my feet because I was cripplingly afraid of in-person interaction with another human, but I still completed that one very slow mile.

What I've learned is that I was creating and reinforcing new neural pathways through tiny, repetitive steps. It was difficult to do at first because my brain was so accustomed to following the deeply engrained pathways that corresponded with my helplessness and self-destruction. But, as it turns out, the brain is an old dog that *can* learn new tricks. The more I flossed, the more I was able to accomplish.

Then, the most interesting thing happened. The triggering incidents still frequently occurred, but I stopped jumping to a craving for suicide or vodka. Instead, my mouth would begin watering for *floss*. I had literally retrained my brain on how I wanted it to react to these stressful events.

I don't think that depression and suicidality should be ignored or avoided by any means. I think all emotions hold deeper meaning and messages for us and should be processed, felt, and released. However, when I was in that knee-deep pool of sticky gunk, I needed to get the hell out of it—or at least find the railing—before I could even consider the option of sorting through and cleaning the muck. That's what flossing became for me: a safety railing to hold onto. It helped me realize that I *did* have somewhat of a hold on my life. Floss gave me hope.

Around this time, I had a conversation with my dad and brother about how unhealthy my lifestyle was. Their primary focus was my consumption of tap water.

I drank lots of water out of the faucet and was dealing with brain fog and headaches and lethargy in addition to the depression. They seemed certain that, if I cut out tap water for two weeks, I'd feel substantially better. They also recommended I do some right-brained activities. They both researched on their own time and sent me recommendations. They said my lifestyle was too logical and too high-strung. (As I write this, years later, I'm heavily nodding in agreement.)

It took a while before I was up to doing the right-brained activities, but I did immediately cut out tap water. I thought they were full of shit, but figured it was worth it to at least humor them. Within days, I felt more clarity. I stopped forgetting what I was talking about in the middle of a sentence.

Therapist recommended I begin taking an anti-depressant. "There's no need to suffer through life," she'd say. I wasn't a fan of taking medication, but I did realize the necessity for some kind of bridge between where I was and the stable ground of sanity. I began taking Wellbutrin, which would help with my severely depleted dopamine neurotransmitters. The medication made my vision fuzzy and caused me to feel very weird, but I continued to take it. It, too, gave me a sense of hope. And, during those years, hope seemed nearly impossible to come by.

~ * ~

Since I had never really been unemployed (even as a kid I had Kool-Aid stands and a pet-sitting business), I decided to busy myself with some form of studying during my time away from a job. I bought The Owner's Manual to the Brain. I learned about sleep and the circadian cycle, which apparently lasts roughly 90 minutes. That's to say that sleeping in 1.5 hour increments is the best way to feel rested when waking up. This is why 7.5 hours of sleep can feel more restful than 8.5 hours. This was fascinating to learn.

At first, I took advantage of it by pushing myself too hard and sleeping very few hours, always making sure each night's sleep was divisible by 1.5

to ensure I completed my sleeping cycles and wouldn't feel groggy in the morning. This worked rather well in the beginning, but depletion soon caught up with me. I was consuming 5-10 servings of coffee a day. And energy drinks. And liquor. And Goodies powder. And Midol. And Wellbutrin. And Adderall.

Within a few weeks, I had my old manager from the FBO reach out to me and offer me a job with whatever schedule I wanted. It was one of those weird examples of letting go of the outcome of a certain situation and having an unexpected opportunity fall into my lap. There was simply no way I could have anticipated the phone call or the offer. I agreed to work part time so that I could focus on school and on self-help.

During my study time, I cracked open Potatoes Not Prozac by Kathleen DesMaisons Ph.D. This introduced me to sugar sensitivity and how sugar sensitive people's brains and bodies react to sugar and alcohol versus the reactions for normal, non-sensitive folks. Reading her words helped me realize that maybe, just maybe, I *wasn't alone*.

In the book, she explains the importance of eating a breakfast with protein within the first hour of waking up, *every single day*. She explains that, if someone doesn't feel hungry for breakfast, it's a telltale sign that this person's system is imbalanced. Once there's a level of trust built with the body, a person will wake up feeling hungry. She breaks the program up into certain steps and recommends not moving on to the following step until the present one is fully integrated. The steps are rather simple, yet profound. I took the recommended program very seriously and, through a combination of Dr. Mike Dow's approach and this one, I lost the "need" to binge eat and to drink alcohol.

I remember the first day I woke up without a hangover. I soon realized that I hadn't consumed any alcohol the night prior which was, quite possibly, the first day in years that this had occurred. I simply didn't think about it. *This was a miracle.* I continued to occasionally drink (and, when I did, I'd make it worth my while and get nice and drunk), but I was no longer regularly consuming 5-10 shots a day.

Prior to my dietary adjustments and research on the brain, I obsessed about and desperately craved alcohol and sugar. When I was drinking a shot, I was planning for (and oftentimes pouring) the next. When I was eating breakfast, I was thinking of what the next meal would entail. My new, healthier lifestyle allowed me to begin experiencing what life was like with stabilized blood sugar and a well-fed brain.

~ * ~

Throughout my existence, and especially as I decreased the amount of numbing substances I consumed, I had many odd experiences. I now know these as paranormal in nature. Before I continue, let me state the following: I am aware that the circumstances I dealt with could have been explained in sensible ways. Trust me, I did the research. I applied intellectual and probable explanations. I worked to convince myself that my unhealthy lifestyle (working and drinking too much and playing and sleeping too little) had starved my brain of its necessary neurotransmitters and, when combined with copious amounts of stress, left me with resulting hallucinations and visualizations. I assumed these were based on repressed memories or previous traumas.

I remember one morning; I awoke to my bed shaking. It was about 3AM. Living in Georgia, I knew an earthquake was unlikely, but was clueless as to what else could have caused such movement. Since I always slept with my nightstand lamp on, I was able to quickly scan the room. Nothing else was shaking. No one else appeared to be there. The bed continued to tremble. This wasn't a gentle rocking back and forth, either. This felt as though two people had the bottom corners of the mattress and box spring and were rapidly moving them in random directions. I closed my eyes, breathed in through my nose and out through my mouth, hoping this anxiety exercise would stop the apparent anxiety-induced hallucinations I was experiencing. The bed still shook.

"Please help me. Please help me." I repeatedly whispered, unsure who I was even addressing.

Gets a little weird here, but keep reading...

The bed went still. I felt my face get hot as my adrenaline levels began their descent. My slow and calm breathing switched to a rapid succession of short breaths as I attempted to process what had just occurred. *Squeeeak.* One of the springs in my bed made a noise that should only accompany the presence of weight. I looked toward the sound in the bottom left corner. I did my best not to blink as I focused my vision on the comforter. *Squeeeak.* The noise happened again. This time, I saw the comforter move in sync with the sounds, forming into the indentations of someone's feet. The indentations continued moving toward me.

I pulled the comforter over my head.

"Dear God or-or Jesus or Allah or—" I started.

Squeeaak.

"--OR WHOEVER. Please help me. Please protect me." I was frantic.

I felt weight next to me in the bed, as if an adult was kneeling by my body. I sensed eyes staring at me, accompanied by a sinister smile. I struggled to breathe the hot air underneath the covers, but I refused to move.

"Dear God! Dear Universe! Please help me now! God help me god help me godhelpmegodhelpmegodhelpme." My voice raised octaves as I pleaded.

I felt a light weight, evenly distributed on top of my body. It got heavier.

"LEAVE ME ALONE!"

The weight vanished. I opened my eyes and shifted my focus around the room, even though my sight was blocked by the blankets. I suppose I was aiming my sensory perception at my surroundings to get some kind of feedback. The bed felt lighter. I no longer sensed a presence near me. I yanked the covers from my face and breathed in fresh air. I frantically glanced around, but saw nothing.

Once my heartrate settled back to normal, my logical sensibility also returned. It first poked fun at the fact that I considered myself agnostic and yet I begged some mystical higher power for help whenever I was in danger. *Hypocritical much?* It said to me. Next, I replayed the scenes of what had occurred, allowing my explanatory mind to fill in the blanks.

This was how I handled every unexplainable circumstance: with logic.

When I experienced the fan turning on and off on its own, for instance, I convinced myself that it was due to the appliance itself being antiquated. The three random fires in the kitchen (two in the dishwasher, one on the electric stove while warming a small pot of water) were because of heat or grease or some obvious chemical reaction of X & Y equating to fire. The terrifying dreams were a way for my subconscious to process and release information attained throughout my day-to-day life. The shaking of my bed awakening me in the middle of the night was because of night tremors or anxiety due to caffeine intake. My seeing parts of the comforter moving toward my body as if under the weight of slow, heavy footprints was wind, or the fan, or because I did not have my glasses on, or because I had watched too many scary movies, or because I had an attention-starved imagination.

First it was because I was young and hormonal. Then I worked too much. Then I was an alcoholic. Then I was unhealthy. The list went on. The excuses continued, and so did the experiences.

I assumed the concepts of good and evil within different realms were creative concepts dreamed up by film and novel writers. God, angels, demons, faeries, and the like— I put all of them under the umbrella of "FICTION." On March 29th, 2014, however, I was forced to re-examine this umbrella, as the ensuing circumstances were nothing short of cinematic phenomena.

and reading...

~ * ~

For years I found the world within my dreams to be far more enjoyable and less painful than what waking life encompassed. As such, I slept. A lot. I took frequent naps to feign off depression, most of which would last through the afternoon, night, and into the next morning. When I awoke on this specific afternoon, I was in a state of semi-paralysis. My body was unable to move, but my conscious mind was present. This was a somewhat common occurrence for me. I had endured many frightening experiences while in such a state. My heartrate increased, attempting to wake my temporarily numbed body with each pulsation. In between the repetitive throbs in my ears, I heard the sound of a lullaby and a little kid's voice.

I was 27 years old at the time and living alone in a 575 square foot apartment. The downstairs neighbor was a mysterious guy who I had only seen a handful of times as he toted his newly-shined golf clubs to his RAV4. He also lived alone. The separation between our living spaces was so thin that I was able to clearly hear his drawn-out yawn every morning at 5AM. If anyone else lived with him, my hypersensitive hearing would have informed me. Hearing anything related to children within our vicinity was far from normal. Yet, this eerily comforting lullaby was coming from my room.

I focused my energy inward, took a deep breath, and pushed it out, successfully forcing my body awake with a slight jerking motion of my head. As I let my eyes adjust to the waking world, I saw a figure sitting on top of my dresser. It was small, see-through, and had edges resembling the waviness of a mirage. This figure was that of a child. I could not physically decipher if it was a girl or a boy. I felt a fondness toward the child, which I did not understand. Soon, fear crept in and took the place of my sleepy weariness. I sat up in my bed, making sure not to blink. The lullaby stopped. Suddenly, the mirage-child darted out of my bedroom. After a rapid allowance of inner turmoil, I followed it.

I grabbed a stiletto (as a weapon) and cautiously walked into the living room. I felt the child's presence in the upper left corner, in between the wall with the wood-burning fireplace and the connecting wall leading to the dusty, covered patio. I squinted in an effort to get a glimpse of the mirage waves again. I heard a loud BOOIIING noise behind me, from across the room. My face flushed with adrenaline as I sprung around to see my computer monitor lighting up from its normal state of darkness. Microsoft Word was open to a blank document. The cursor was blinking.

"This is happening," I said aloud. "This is actually happening."

I felt a sensation that I hadn't experienced in over a decade as tingles of wonder and curiosity danced in my stomach and across my skin.

My logical mind quickly interjected, grabbing the excited butterfly sensation by its throat, and told me I'd likely left Microsoft Word open during my last failed attempt at writing. *Then how did the monitor turn on?* I thought. There was silence in return. Some butterflies escaped the grip of my logic, allowing my childlike curiosity to prevail.

"Do… You want me to write?" I asked aloud.

An 8 1/2" x 11" sheet of paper fell from its home on the wall above my desk, as if it had been batted down. It was one of the motivational pieces I kept up in an effort to convince myself to write. It was March and it was chilly, but I rarely, if ever, used the heat. I quickly confirmed that there was no air conditioning, heat, or open window to create a draft. Still, a piece of paper that had been secured to the wall had fallen directly after I delivered a question.

I took this as a yes.

I sat down at the desk.

I placed my fingers on the appropriate keys.

I began writing.

(Times New Roman denotes the trance typing. The responses are italicized. The narrative of the event remains in this Courier New font.)

What is it that you need to say?
Jennifer was a child once. She was a child but she doesnt remember it.

I felt my intellect fighting me, telling me I was making this up. My heart believed otherwise. I adjusted the font to size 4, making it impossible to read what was being typed. I closed my eyes, hoping this would give my heart more reign than my brain.

Clear your mind Let us speak
Who is us?
Michael

My fingers moved to press more keys, but I pulled my hands away. *Michael,* I thought. I went through the different interactions I'd had within the last week, desperate to find a person named Michael. This would be a logical reason for his name to be in the forefront of my mind. I recalled a few encounters with strangers named Michael, but that was it.

This is my imagination, right? I have a strong imagination.
Clear your mind. Just let us speak Let go of inhibitions Let go of your wrists and tension

I noticed that I'd been typing differently. I have always typed with only my pointer and middle fingers. Typing the "correct" way felt awkward when I attempted it, so I usually stuck to my chicken-peck style. However, during these apparent responses, my ring and pinkie fingers joined.

I am not trying to be needy. I just want clarity. What am I supposed to do? Who is this presence?
Stop worrying you will be fine you are here for a purpose stop thinking
My whole life I've felt different.
you are different
Does that make me selfish? I just feel special. Special in a way where there's more. There's more than the normal societal influence that guides most sheep throughout life. That is not meant for me. When I go on that pathway it leads me to depression and darkness and anger and sadness and drinking and numbness.
Alcohol
Is poison

I felt a sinking sensation in my gut as these words were typed. The last twelve months had held a handful of very difficult situations, which were always accompanied by liquor.

It is poison to my mind and I know that. The mistakes I've made came when alcohol was present.
Alcohol numbs your chances of speaking with us. Alcohol and drugs numb your senses. You need your senses.

I concentrated on my breath, attempting to remain focused.

I'm present in this moment and that is rare. It is rare. How do I get better?
You are. Don't worry about going faster. You always want to go faster and in doing so you slow yourself down by not listening right now. If you listened. Listened. Listened. To your world now you would hear us from the other world.

The phrase "other world" caused my Inner Critic to poke me with thoughts of *See? You're clearly making this up. The OTHER WORLD... Really?! Can you get any more cliché?*

Other world… isn't that just some term I read on the internet?
Yes but it is more than that.

This response did not reach my Censor's expectations for a believable argument. My mind rumbled as my patterned way of thinking fought to expose the loopholes within the responses.

Stop being frustrated with yourself it makes it harder for us to communicate
Keep your eyes closed. That's a vibration you feel side to side. Feel things around you to ground yourself.

My perspective zoomed out momentarily as I imagined an acquaintance viewing this ordeal. *As if they don't already think I'm crazy,* I thought.

Embarrassment will get you nowhere stop worrying about spelling errors and embarrassment stop worrying all of the worrying is pointless and will get you nowhere.
But I'm trying.
We understand that you're trying but you need to slow down
How will I be successful if I slow down?
Hahahahaha.. you don't yet understand Listen to your heart. The stars. You are smarter than you give yourself credit for. You're on the right path. Continue to be kind. Kindness will set you free.
Free from what?
Free from your consciousness and your hatred of yourself.

"Hatred" first seemed too harsh of a word to describe how I felt toward myself, but I quickly realized that the harshness fell under the Truth Hurts category of emotional responses. I had only recently begun being kind to myself, shifting my diet to healthier options and subsequently cutting back on liquor, but I still was far from supportive of myself. *Even now,* I thought, *I am judging every word that is written.* In coming to terms with this self-hatred, I decided to set it aside for the remainder of the present conversation. *Maybe,* I thought, *just maybe this is valid. Maybe this is real. How can I know if I keep fighting it?* I let go of the need to appear sane or correct or put-together. I typed.

> I feel disappointed in myself often, even though I feel like I am doing my best. Even there I said "like" and it frustrated me because I hate using that word.
> *As you concentrate on these minor things you consider flaws you are missing the world that is passing you by the the stars in the sky and the moon and the orbiting moon and the space the uninhibited void that is the universe. It is so free and beautiful and you will be here again one day and you will inhabit another body. It took you longer than we thought.*
> Longer for what?
> *To find us.*
> Who is us? I want to type archangels but I don't even know what that means.
> *Research it.*
> Does it have to do with god?

I surprised myself when I typed the word god. I had previously created a well-traveled path around the word by consistently avoiding any religious terminology.

> *Yes.*
> Is god as everyone popularly knows him?
> *You say him why?*
> Society.
> *Ah. Society. The very society you are attempting to not conform to yet you have assigned a gender to something that is genderless. It is an overarching creation of lust and love and growing freedom and just breathe. Breathe. Music will help your mind calm. Put on the music.*

Which song? Show me which song and give me a sign.
Is this not sign enough?
No. It isn't that I do not trust *you* it is that I have struggles trusting myself. My conscious mind, I mean. My subconscious is beautiful and I want to learn to let it free more frequently.
You should why aren't you what is stopping you?
Me. I am stopping me. Fear is stopping me. Fear. Is there a song about fear?

I opened my phone's music library and searched for the right song. I found myself under the artist Nine Inch Nails. I randomly chose the song The Downward Spiral, but quickly felt pulled to type again.

There is negativity out there and it is attracted to you.
WHY?
Because you are vulnerable in this state. You've gotten stronger. Stronger and no longer drunk no longer intoxicated beyond the point of recognition. We reached out to you before and gave you signs. You even recognized some but promptly discounted them or forgot them due to memory loss instilled upon you by drinking.

Always one for answers and reasoning, I decided to push for more pointed information.

What is this about?
You.
What about me?
Grew up way too fast and now there's everything to believe in because you are different

A sensation of nausea overtook my body as it rocked steadily side to side, at no effort of my own. My physical energy waned.

Shakiness is normal at first. it will get better easier clearer. concentrate on the feeling in the back of your neck at the base of your skull. Breathe breathe breathe. Weakness is normal too physically you may feel drained but emotionally stronger than ever which is what you need it is where you lack we will be back we are always here you just need to follow the signs.
Hard to tell what the signs are.

yes because you aren't paying attention you are always in your phone get into nature go into mature nature nature and you will find find signs there there will be something you see we will show you

Ok...

I know you want to know who we are and who the little girl in your apartment is.

Who is she?

The little girl in your apartment is the little girl in your head.

This statement prompted a flurry of images into my mind as I imagined how doctors would interpret the current two-way conversation I was seemingly having with myself. *No, Doc. I'm not talking to myself. I'm talking to an Archangel named Michael. And it's okay! The thing I saw on my dresser wasn't necessarily a ghost. It was a representation of my inner child. You see, Doc, I am scattered. I am so disconnected that the inner parts of myself have become disjointed and are having to get my attention in drastic ways.*

I cradled my forehead with my palms, which quickly moved back to the keyboard.

YOU SIMPLY NEED TO REMOVE YOURSELF FROM YOUR HEAD AND ALLOW YOURSELF, YOUR CURRENT SELF, TO EXPERIENCE THIS LIFETIME. DON'T IGNORE THE SIGNS.

I need more signs. Lightning bold signs, if you will. I need proof. Skepticism.

Share your writing with the world. It is an eye into your soul. Feel the weightlessness in your chest and body right now and imagine the freedom that can be felt if you fulfill what you are here to do.

Which is? Sorry.

The truth Is simple. You will save the souls of others.

I pushed away from the keyboard and said a few choice cuss words aloud. *Great,* I thought. *There are two options here. One, I am legitimately insane and am making all of this up unbeknownst to myself, which is indicative of I don't know how many disorders. Or two, there really is an Archangel named Michael who is SOMEHOW typing through me, which would mean I am supposed to use my writing to save the souls of others.* Yea. Sure. Simple enough.

I heard creaking in the ceiling of my apartment. I lived on the top floor, so the sound could not be attributed to upstairs neighbors. I hoped it was a squirrel or raccoon.

You needn't have fear. You are stronger than them now. You will feel less of the negative spirits and you will feel more of the positive ones.
Spirits. Is that my conscious mind coming up with that word or is it something else?
let us us speak
I'm trying

My logical mind found its way to the conversation and filled me in on its reasoning for what was happening. *There was likely something traumatic that happened to you and you created this other part of you so you could talk it out,* it convincingly told me.

Yes there was Abuse that went deeper than you remember and when you're strong enough we will show you but you must learn the art of forgiveness first
There are two sides to every person and some have more.,. Some have more than two sides. More than five senses. More than six. You are to relax and let your sides work together rather than against each other.
How do I know when to listen to these sides?
easy answer and you know which is correct in every instance but you are too busy with thinking of the future or the past
How do I fight off the darkness?
Write.
Share.
It will come to you but your intuition and inspiration are being trumped by your conscious insecurities. Find the time make the time to write like you say you will and like you think about doing. Imagine the success and it will follow. Put it into your heart and make that picture your metaphorical dangling carrot though you will not hunger for much longer.
Why let me suffer when I have suffered so deeply and felt so alone and afraid and dark?
You need to fight through darkness on your own accord to show the strength of your soul on this earth. It needs to build a shield and your shield has become very thick. Your vulnerability scares you and you run and get lost. When youre lost, you need a map back to this. You need to talk to us more. The communication will become clearer. Stop concentrating on the pain the pain is the darkness anything that fights against you doing what you know you are meant to do is the darkness

I wondered if there were others experiencing anything similar to this and if there was a support group or a step-by-step guidebook to help me with comprehension or give me some glimmer of hope that I was still sane. I heard more creaking, as if wood was bending underneath immense weight.

Yes, there are others. There are others. They hide themselves.
Stay off the internet and use your intuition instead
How do I know the difference between intuition and imagination? I just want to know what I am supposed to follow.
youll feel in your heart and in your fingertips what to follow. You will know the difference. But there will still be struggle.,. you are going to have down moments but this connection between us and between you and your soul and your mind and heart is going to be so much stronger as a result.
How do I speak with a presence?
This way. You need to type or write. That is your gift. Words. Words are your gift. It is something your parents' souls knew. From a past life.
They were my parents in a past life too?
Souls never leave each other. They wait in the universe amidst the stars and they wait for the rest of the family and loved ones to join. Then they go on into a new set of bodies, trying again. And again. To get it right.

Whoa, I thought, *this is some heavy shit.* I quickly checked in with my Censor, wondering why it wasn't fighting these claims. It, too, was intrigued. It had no correlation between when I had heard or read something similar. I continued.

What is the purpose? And who is it that I hear above me?
That is us. We are not harmful. We are not going to hurt you and that presence should make you feel safe. We are here to protect you and help guild you. Your roots are deep and strong enough and your scars are thick enough to protect you from the temptation of darkness and evil, apathy and laziness and darkness and boredom.
What is the darkness?
It wants what it can't have. It comes across as other things. Sweetness. Presents. Nice words. It will attach to things that cause you so much pain. Your first concentration must be to gain forgiveness toward these people these sheep these bodies these shells that have hurt you. work to find a balance inside you. Work to keep your heartrate the same and your anxiety level low.

I suddenly felt exhausted, as though I was hungover. I struggled to focus my vision.

You are getting tired. You mustn't sp[rint through this, Jennifer ANnn. ' Find peace. Follow the dots.
You will save people from suicide. From depression. You will save people from themselves. You will find your following and they will love you but more importantly you will help them love themselves. Do not worry about money it will come. Put it into the universe and it will come.
How do I know if I will be successful?
you don't. You don't know. You believe. You ask for help when you need it and you prepare to be guided through life by your soul and its intuitions and its butterflies and moths.
Youre getting tired. Go take care of your responsibilities. Take care of your outer responsibilities so that you can be less inwardly inhibited.
We are here. We are here. Our names will come to you soon. I am Michael. We are the ones who guide you. In an effort to lead you away from the darkness that is within your genes. You are an orb. You are a receptacle you are a sponge. A sponge that, if not filled with positivity and happiness and perspective and soul work, will be filled with negativity.
You need to create. Finish your memoir. Finish it and it will be published.
Stay healthy and strong. Be outside. Live. Live this life You have many more to come, but this life has the potential to yield amazing results.
I feel as though I'm typing that from my conscious mind in an effort to justify everything. *That's your conscious mind. It is its job to make you wonder and second guess.*
It is your soul's job to know.
It knows. Let is speak.
It is bruised and it is scarred. Its voice is quiet and meek. But it will be worth it if you listen.
Go. let go and be free.
Go.

My hands remained in their places, hovering just above the face of the keys, awaiting direction. I waited for more typing. Nothing happened. I felt myself slowly descend back into my body, as if I'd boon floating in a meditative state for the past hour. I blinked repeatedly in an effort to moisten my eyes, which were dry from having stared at the white screen with such straining curiosity. I tried to clearly define what had just happened, but struggled to recall anything that was said. I selected all text within the document and adjusted the font to a legible size. I scrolled to the top. I began reading.

I was admittedly terrified and confused by what had happened. I also felt this grumble of excitement in my belly. Of *what if?* There had always been this part of me that desperately craved something *more* out of life. Even though I was a left-brained logic-based atheist who demanded evidence as proof of any claim, I still hoped life was more magical than what I believed. There was always that little glimmer of wonder. Of curiosity.

Was it possible that this information was true? That I was here to help save others from depression? Was that why I had so heavily dealt with it, so I could know their pain?

Or was I somehow making all of this stuff up in order to feel more important than I really was?

Or was I bat-shit crazy and in need of stronger medication or padded walls?

At first, I told no one of this encounter.

Who could I tell? I thought, *What would I say? What if they thought I was crazy? Maybe they'd be right.*

Honestly, I wasn't sure which outcome I most wanted. I think that admitting insanity would have been an easier route, I'll tell you that much.

What was typed from/through me resonated deeply, on what I now know as an energetic and even cellular level. Something was unlocked within me. We will call this my official aha moment. Although it took many more read-throughs and considerations to put the information into action, this was the undoubtedly the turning point in my life. It was a paradigm shift that I in no way anticipated.

On April 5th, 2014, I had my last sip of alcohol. It was a swig of chilled Grey Goose vodka directly out of the bottle before leaving a short beach trip I'd been on with the guy I was dating. We'll call him Banker. I actually stopped drinking before the trip

and had a few days sober. That's when I realized that the enjoyment and laughter I'd experienced with Banker were both attached to the presence of liquor in my system. I bought a small-ish bottle of Grey Goose on our first beach day in an effort to increase our fun. He was a great guy, but I knew in my heart that this relationship would not coincide with my sobriety.

Something weird started to happen when drinking. I no longer enjoyed the way alcohol made me feel. The love of losing my grip on reality had become obsolete, seemingly overnight. Sure, I'd been working for months to balance my brain chemistry so I could get my binge eating and alcohol drinking under control, but this felt more like a switch had been flipped.

Once back home, I decided to tell Banker about the conversation with this supposed Archangel Michael. (Even to this day, the skeptical part of me is still like, "What if it *wasn't* an archangel?" And I'm like, "Dude, I don't care if it was Santa Claus or telepathy from a stink bug; what was said is profound. The end.") I began reading the document to him, skipping a few parts that felt too out-there to share. I could sense his energy shifting as I read the document aloud.

"That's really weird, Jen. Kind of freaky," he finally said.

"Yea," I said. I started to agree with the voice in my head that assumed I was crazy. *You're not special,* it said. *You just want to think you're special, so you created this alternate reality.*

There was silence, which was rather uncomfortable without the aid of vodka.

"What are you thinking?" I asked.

"I'm honestly scared."

"Scared of what?"

"I dunno'. I'm scared I'm gonna' wake up to you standing by the bed with an ax."

"You don't even own an ax."

"Yea but you get what I mean."

"No, I don't," I responded. "How does all of this," I motioned to the laptop screen, "lead you to think *that*?"

He went on to tell a story of when he was younger and his mom forced him to church. He saw a little girl possessed by *something* and speaking in different languages and stuff. His mom made him cover his ears and look the other way, so he never got to see what happened to her. My situation triggered that memory and its corresponding fear and confusion.

This was one of a handful of people who reacted in such a manner toward my spiritual awakening. I dealt with squinty eyes, skepticism, and disbelief in response to the account of my experiences. Looking back, I'm able to see that I was attracting these people to my life because I, myself, was a skeptic who was struggling to believe in my own experiences.

I ended things with Banker a few weeks later, in an admittedly abrupt fashion. I knew in my bones that it was the right thing to do. I did it via email, which guaranteed the least amount of confrontation. (And, within a few weeks, I was dating Actor. Remember the baton tendency? Yea…) I'm not proud of how I handled this (or many) situations in my past, but I also have learned to accept them. I know I was doing the best I could from my level of awareness.

At that time in my life, speaking to someone in person about stressful topics put me into a blue screen, where my brain would become overloaded with all of the possible outcomes and meanings and feelings, and I'd shut down. Writing felt safer. Easier. (Honestly, it still does. I have come a long way, though, and can now stumble my way through stressful conversations in real life. Emphasis on *stumble.*) Finding the balance with my writing has been (and continues to be) a challenge. It is so much easier for me to say, *I'm a writer; speaking aloud is simply hard for me,* than it is for me to push myself to improve my skills with verbal expression.

I've found that, even though vulnerable verbal expression may still bring up anxious feelings and a tendency toward over-analysis, it also yields *huge* breakthroughs. Further, the more I share my true thoughts and feelings real-time and aloud, the clearer and more aligned my writing becomes. I'm able to get honest with myself and uncover what I *really* want to say.

~ * ~

Transitioning into my chapter of spirituality was a fast, bumpy ride. I've had people refer to my experience as a spontaneous spiritual awakening. I've since met others who've experienced similar awakenings through their sobriety. It makes sense, really; by discontinuing the numbing act of ingesting intoxicants, we begin to hear the subtle voice of our intuition. We start feeling a strong inner pull and push, directing us where to go. I don't think sobriety is the only way to this type of spiritual growth, to be clear, but I do believe that sobriety guarantees some form of awakening.

I decided to start doing "spiritual things." I viewed life in a compartmentalized way and figured that, in order to be spiritual, I needed to *act* spiritual. My first step was to incorporate meditation. This was a challenge in itself, since meditation had always resonated with me as something only spiritual weirdos did. It made no sense to me. *Why sit in silence for extended periods of time when we instead could be taking action steps?* I thought people who prayed were too lazy to take action, and I applied this judgment to those who meditated as well. Also, to be honest, I thought meditation was only for specific cultures. This makes me giggle now.

I was rule-oriented. I enjoyed following directions in order to take part in activities in the most efficient and correct manner. I didn't like learning; I enjoyed having learned. I wanted to *know* how to meditate. I wanted to already be good at it, if one could even be good at such an abstract act. *Take me from victimizing depressed person to a floating monk in one meditation, please!*

Beginning to embrace the spiritual weirdo within, I decided to give it a try. Notice I said "decided." I made the conscious decision to *soon begin* this practice, but it took me another month or so to actually take part in it. I am unsure of what I was so hesitant about. Change, perhaps.

Something as foreign as meditation was scary, especially since it seemed to be accompanied by such phrases as "quieting the mind" and "finding comfort in silence." Silence freaked me the hell out. I rarely let silent moments happen during conversations. They felt awkward and thick with tension and nervousness, even more so with the amplifier of sobriety. And quieting the mind? I remember thinking, *Is that even possible? Clearly these folks don't know my mind. I should get a handicap or something.* I had a tendency to use my "being highly intelligent" as a silent excuse for a *lot* of behavior. *I'm too intelligent to quiet my mind. I have more thoughts than most.*

I woke up pre-alarm one morning, which was a miracle in itself. Previously being one to sleep for 10-16 hours a day and still feel exhausted, it was a refreshing adjustment to actually want to wake up. I checked my emails on my phone out of my obsessive need to get rid of those annoying little red notification bubbles near the email app. I was enjoying the rhythmic motion of swiping to the left, hitting the archive button, swiping to the left, hitting the archive button, when a specific email interrupted my archive flow. It held a word in the subject line which grabbed my focus: meditation. Within the email lay a link to a site that gave step by step instructions on how to meditate.

I sat on my covered back porch, which rarely received attention from me. Its primary use had been to house Actor while he inhaled his addiction of choice: Camel cigarettes. I sat with my legs crossed and back straight, as recommended by the website. I concentrated on my breathing, then forgot to concentrate on my breathing, then reminded myself to concentrate on my breathing, then promptly forgot. Something as innate as my lungs sucking in and dispelling air is something I took for granted. My conscious mind was like, *Yea. Breathing. Cool. I already know how this works. What's next?*

In quintessential Jen fashion, I read every line of the directions and applied them exactly. The instructions introduced me to the seven main energy centers called chakras, the knowledge of which increased my spiritual weirdometer. I did the recommended visualizations, the deep and slow breathing, and focused on my physical body rather than my mind. It was about a 45-minute meditation. I don't think I ever officially made it into what I now deem a meditative state, but I definitely made progress by sitting alone with myself and focusing my energy inward.

I dealt with lots of weird stuff when meditating. At first, I would wobble back and forth a lot or move in a repetitive rotation. Neither of these were conscious choices; they happened seemingly on their own. I also experienced headaches and irritability when coming out of a meditative state. I found my way to binaural beats and isochronic tones, both of which helped me to actually get to a quieted frame of mind and get lost in this other world of what I now know as no-mind.

The headaches are what first prompted me to utilize imagination. A friend explained that a transition may be helpful. Rather than going from a seated, meditative state into abruptly standing and continuing with my day, he recommended that I create a place in my mind to transition in and out of this state. He said to count from ten as I went in and count *to* ten as I came out. This transitional area, which I still use to this day, is behind an imaginary bookshelf. The book I pull down is "Where the Wild Things Are," which opens to a secret passageway filled with water and flowers. The flowers are always different. During one session, I saw a door toward the end of my scenic waterway. I imagined myself wading through the water and climbing the steps to this door. I opened it and on the other side was a beautiful field with a huge weeping willow tree with multi-colored leaves.

My visions become clearer and more vivid each day, as did my hearing. While lying in bed at night,

I'd hear people chattering as if they were in the upstairs apartment—only, there was no upstairs apartment. Research told me this was likely my group of "spirit guides," a concept that was initially hard for me to grasp. Admittedly, there are still times when I question the existence of such spirits, even though I've had countless experiences showing me that they do, in fact, exist. We live in a world where seeing is believing. In order to believe in something, we demand physical proof.

It's funny to me now. There are so many parts of life we simply don't question, even though we don't understand how they work. For example, most people probably can't explain how cell phones or gravity or love works, but they just *know* it exists. But things like intuitive communication and earthbound spirits and a group of supportive spirit guides for each person? *NONSENSE. SHOW ME EVIDENCE.*

I've found that, in order to not run myself in circles while attempting to understand certain things, I have to suspend disbelief. When watching a Harry Potter movie, for example, we go in with disbelief suspended. We accept the world for what it is rather than questioning it and demanding evidence. Sure; it's a fictitious movie depicting a magical world. However, do you think the muggles of that world knew of the magic within it? Or did they just "know" that life was limited, boring, scripted, and only legitimate with accompanying physical evidence? Can you admit that it is at least *possible* that we, too, live in a magical world? I'm telling you; inviting in this energy of possibility will subsequently increase the amount of synchronicity in anyone's life.

My argument is that maybe, just maybe, our human consciousness is not able to encompass just how expansive and miraculous our very existence is. It's easier for us to focus on what we can see and what is societally appropriate to believe. I've been privileged with a two-year spiritual safari that has repeatedly taken my breath away by presenting to me situations I only thought possible in fictitious worlds created by writers. I've now gotten to a point where, when people ask me whether or not I think something exists, I say: "Who am I to say what does and doesn't exist? There is so much more out there than what's in my awareness, and I'd prefer to believe that the world we live in is entirely more magical than we can grasp."

~ * ~

I so badly wanted to meet my spirit guides. I didn't really know what spirit guides were, but I wanted to physically see them. I wanted proof that they were real. I did a lot of Googling during the first parts of my awakening. I did much digging in an effort to find a morsel of evidence proving that what I was experiencing was normal. Or, if these experiences were proof of my being crazy, I wanted to find other similar crazies to whom I could relate.

Throughout my endeavors, I mostly discovered a lot of poorly designed websites. Most of the stuff I read consisted of old blog entries, laden with spelling errors. Although I'd have previously hit the back button upon reading the second spelling error of a webpage, I powered through and concentrated on the content. After all, I didn't know where else to look. (I would love to get a hold of my Google search history from that period of time.)

I read about spirit guides and what they were. I received mixed information, as usual. Some people said spirit guides would come and go throughout life. Other people claimed that the guides stayed from birth. Others, still, said we all have one main guide and then plenty of guides for other aspects of our lives. For instance, if a person is a snowboarder, there would be a corresponding snowboarding guide. I chuckled when I first read about this. It made me think of the 1994 movie Angels in the Outfield.

Keep in mind, I was reading all of this from a left-brained mindset. I was trying so hard to apply logic. I began studying quantum physics in an effort to gain an understanding of some kind. I wanted a foundation to build upon.

I also wanted to see my pucking spirit guides. That, in my mind, was the only way I could know they were real.

"If you exist, show yourself to me," I would say aloud, as if they were merely hiding behind a wall waiting to be summoned.

I tried special baths, special meditations, and even special diets in an effort to reach my spirit guides. I attempted automatic writing to communicate with them. (This is similar to the stream of consciousness writing I mentioned earlier. I write for a certain amount of time without stopping. Even if I have to repeat the same sentence five times, I repeat it rather than stopping. Even if what comes through makes no sense, I keep writing. This allows the creative and intuitive flow to come through.) The information I received was that one spirit guide's name started with a J and the other with an A, though I figured I was likely making both of those up.

Looking back, I realize that I was relying on my dulled regular senses for these interactions. Anything related to the spiritual realm is far easier to experience using the hyper-sensitive sixth sense(s) we all have. Y'know. Intuition. It's not something to be forced into existence. It's something that already exists and is available at all times; all one must do is let go and allow. Simple, yet far from easy.

Work and school and relationship with Actor were all going well. I was regularly journaling about my meditations and taking notes from what websites seemed somewhat trustworthy. I had a regular exercise regimen. I felt more stable than I'd ever been. And still, I felt a need for more. More knowledge. More meditation. More reading. More healing. And certainly more hearing and seeing.

~ * ~

One day, while working at the front desk of the FBO, I saw a black bird land on the rod iron chair, which resided on the sidewalk leading up to the tarmac. The bird looked at me. We kept eye contact. Unsure if it was a crow or a raven, I Googled the difference between the two, discovering that it was indeed a raven, which had always been a favorite animal of mine. I then looked up the spiritual significance of a raven. Right as I was reading about "the need for change," I heard a one-syllable word clearly in my head: *Quit.*

I looked up at the raven, who remained steady.

Quit?! Like, quit here? This job? I thought back to the bird.

You need a change. Quit. Heal. Recover. Write, I heard in response.

And so I did. I put in my two weeks' notice. Because a raven told me to. My last day was on July 13th, 2014.

Sure, I was skeptical. But the majority of me was saying "Why not?" There was still the inner craving for life being more magical than I'd previously believed. Additionally, had I ignored the call of this raven, I'd have always wondered *what if.*

I utilized my time away from professional work as an opportunity to fully immerse myself in personal work. I would wake up at 5-5:30AM in order to meditate, read, and write out positive affirmations and intentions. (The one I repeated the most was something along the lines of: "I am a NY Times Best-selling author. My writing heals myself and others.") I would exercise. I'd also be sure to eat breakfast within the first hour of waking up, per the step from Potatoes, Not Prozac.

Through a professor's recommendation, I began reading books by Deepak Chopra. I would read for hours, highlighting and making notes, soaking everything in. I found some of his stuff a little too out-there for me at the time, but he clearly seemed to know what he was talking about.

My sessions with Therapist changed. The longer I was away from drugs and alcohol, the more intuitively sensitive I was becoming. In sessions, I'd be able to tune into her reactions and emotions. One afternoon that I met with her, I suddenly knew she'd been through a divorce and was mentally and emotionally exhausted. Perhaps my growing imagination created this reality. Or perhaps it was true. I soon realized that the guidance I needed was spiritual, not mental.

I had been researching about the power of intention and stating my wants and needs for the Universe. So, on a large post-it note, I wrote, "I need a spiritual mentor." The post-it note remained propped up to the left of my apartment's fireplace.

~ * ~

A week later, when interviewing a woman for Kennesaw State University's Coming Out Monologues, my request was answered. Toward the end of my sit-down meeting with Painter, who is a phenomenal artist, she mentioned something about energy.

"I don't know if you believe in all of that stuff, but I do," she said.

I was immediately giddy that a real life human being was talking to me about energy, since it was something I felt hesitant to bring up in normal conversation. (It's funny, really, because *everything* is energy. This is a fact. And yet, bringing it up in conversation frequently results in awkward silences and disbelief.) I read about it on websites and had been reading spiritual books, but I'd yet to communicate about this stuff with someone aside from Actor. I told Painter that I had recently begun a sort of spiritual awakening.

"Have you ever done reiki?" She asked.

"No. What is reiki?" I inched my phone toward her to be sure the recording app would pick up everything she said.

"Well, it has to do with energy."

"I'm all about it!" I exclaimed.

"Me too. I'm all about it. I have a reiki master I go to."

"What is that?"

"Reiki? It's energy work."

I wrote "rakey" in the top right corner of my interview notes, spelling it based on how she was saying it.

"R-e-i-k-i," Painter said when she saw me writing. "Her name is Mentor, and here is her number."

I scribbled down the information in the margin of my notes.

"What does she do? How does it work?" I asked.

"You become a reiki master by learning different kinds of energy work. I don't know if there's different levels or whatever… But basically you go to the person's home, you lay on the person's massage table—fully clothed—on your back. And you have to go in with your mind quiet… And your mind open… And zero expectations. And she's magical, honestly. The first time I ever had it, I saw color, I felt vibration, and I was in a very deep what I guess you'd call a hypnotic state. I felt like I was sinking into the table. There's not much touch. It's really more of… Like… She places little trinkets and things on you. And afterward she's like, *here's some oil to help ground you. Keep this particular rock in your pocket.*"

"That is awesome!" I exclaimed.

"Yea," she said. "It is. Shit like this has been done for a *lot* of years. It obviously works. Energy is a real thing. If someone's in a bad mood and you walk in and you're like… *Why do I feel weird? Why am I suddenly in a bad mood?* That's energy. THAT SHIT'S, LIKE, REAL."

"Definitely," I said.

"She's a very grounded person. I call her Mother Earth because she's this amazing, magical woman."

"I'm amped. I've recently gotten to a point where I'm not getting much from a therapist anymore because it seems to be all of this surface talk. And I'm to the point now where I'm able to pick up on my therapist's energy and I'm like, 'You are not even into this today… And I'm paying you $100.'"

"Exactly," she said. "More and more people are into this energy stuff. I believe it to be true because I've experienced it. It's incredible and I'm all about people trying new experiences."

"I am literally going to call her as soon as I leave here."

She laughed. "Good!"

And that's precisely what I did. I wrapped up the interview and, once Painter's front door was closed, I sprinted to my car and called Mentor. I left her a voice message that was, in typical Jen fashion, *really* long and detailed. I explained the work I'd been doing and how I'd recently quit my job and how all of these synchronistic things were happening, including how I got her information. She called me back within the hour and we set up an appointment for the following Thursday.

~ * ~

I'm not sure what I expected Mentor to look like. I think I sort of anticipated an 80-year-old lady with a head wrap and a crystal ball with eerie music and a fog machine going. That Thursday, I parked outside of her house and walked toward her porch. I saw her cat lying on the top step. He lifted his head and looked into my eyes. I immediately heard the thought in my head of:

May I help you?

I glanced around and then back into the cat's eyes.

Can you hear me? I consciously thought. Again, without a break for thinking time, I heard the thought:

Can't you see that I'm busy?

He put his head back down and closed his eyes. I giggled, unsure if my imaginative mind was creating the dialogue or if it was real. Mentor opened the front door.

"Hi, Jennifer! Come on in!" Her voice was soft, yet strong, and very welcoming. She was much younger than I'd anticipated. I guessed she was in her mid-thirties. She had blonde hair and was the embodiment of a beach babe version of Mother Earth.

"It's so nice to meet you!" I said as we hugged.

"You too!" she said. I walked in and sat across from her on her sofa.

"So, you're an animal communicator."

"I… What?" I had this feeling of, *Oh god she can see me!*

"An animal communicator. I saw you communicating with Bojangles. He is quite the greeter."

"I didn't know that's what I was doing. I figured I was just making up thoughts in my head."

She smiled and shook her head no.

"But, um…" I continued. "When I walked up he said—at least I think he said— 'May I help you? I'm busy.'"

She smiled a genuine, loving smile that I would grow even more fond of as we got to know each other.

"You weren't making it up. That's exactly his personality. Holier than thou." She said.

I was shocked that this woman—WHO WASN'T EVEN HOLDING A CRYSTAL BALL AND DID NOT HAVE A FOG MACHINE GOING IN HER HOUSE—was looking at me like I was normal for having a telepathic conversation with a cat. My face ached because of how much I was smiling.

The session itself was a bizarre experience. She played relaxing music and lightly touched or hovered her hands over my main chakras. I went in and out of a meditative state, which was an exciting accomplishment for me. My thoughts did continue snapping me out of it, but they were calmer than usual. I experienced a lot of visuals in what I now know as my third eye, or my mind's eye. I specifically remember seeing goldfish from a bird's eye view. They were eating flakes of fish food. I also saw my horse and a variety of colors. The physical sensations were amazing, too. I could feel energy somehow pulsating from her hands and being absorbed into my body. When the session was done, I felt calm and very present, as if I'd been gently pulled back into my body.

What really wowed me were her session notes. First, she told me she met two of my guides. My guardian angel, she said, was Jeremiel, and one of my spirit guide's names was Aurelia. (That explains my J and A I received from my earlier attempts at communication.) She then told me that Archangel Michael was heavily present with me. I had a minor freak-out moment when she said this, considering what had happened in March. I was finally receiving the validation I had been desperately craving.

She said she was in my life to teach me the fundamentals and that I'd sky rocket afterward. She said I was a channel. I had no idea what that meant at the time, but I nodded my head and took notes like a good little student. She said she saw me with a popular YouTube channel and speaking in front of people. She also mentioned a book. I'd like to think it was this book. She told me that I had spent many lifetimes preparing for this one and that this was likely my last lifetime on earth. (I still believe this to be true. I don't know how else to explain it aside from *knowing* it deep down. It resonates on a level beyond intellect.)

On the drive home, the Google maps app on my phone took me on a different route than the way I had driven to Mentor's house. At one point, I stopped at a stop sign, glanced to my left, and saw the following:

Yea. It's a painting of a bird's eye view of goldfishies with flakes of fish food. Just like I'd seen during my reiki session. It resides on a wall on a street in Atlanta that I'd never before driven on (and was done by an artist named Brandon Sadler). This was one of those "whoa" moments where life showed me a hint of how magical it can be.

Mentor and I scheduled training sessions and a Reiki Level One attunement. In the training, I learned more about the seven main chakras of the human energy field and was introduced to crystals and stones. She started me on a book called Energy Medicine by Donna Eden, which is deliciously nutrient-dense (as in, lots of information). Although Mentor and I are no longer close, I still deeply cherish her and everything she taught me. She is the one who helped guide me on my journey into this place called my "heart space," whereas previously my comfort and confidence stemmed from over-indulgence of my mind. It has been (and still is) a messy and challenging journey, but one that has yielded immense growth. As I've come to find out, the mind is simply one tool that we can choose to utilize; it needn't be active at all times.

~ * ~

One afternoon around this time, I was sitting at my tree at Swift Cantrell Park in Kennesaw, Georgia. I don't actually own the tree, but I feel that our bond is unlike any other's. It was October and the leaves were beginning to change. I sat beneath the tree listening to the entirety of a Mumford & Sons album while doodling. This was a task recommended by Julia Cameron in The Artist's Way: listen to a favorite album and doodle.

While doodling under my tree, a squirrel scurried by. I looked up at said squirrel and very clearly heard:

No title.

Hearing Steve the Squirrel didn't shock me. I mean, it likely would have if I hadn't have quit my corporate job three months prior due to a raven telling me that I needed change. All things considered, this animal talking thing was rather normal.

STEVE

(I have decided that all squirrels are named Steve. In fact, I like to imagine that there is only ONE squirrel in the whole world and the other squirrels we see are holographic representations of the original Steve. And all he's doing is searching for Sally the squirrel. Or another Steve, if that's his preference.) (No, I don't actually believe this. It's just a fun game I play with myself. I find it necessary to clarify this because sometimes sarcasm is hard to interpret via written word. Especially in a book of truth.)

After this note from Steve, I went into a writing frenzy of all sorts of ideas about this titleless book. Next, I decided it wouldn't have page numbers. Also, it wouldn't have headings or sub-headings. *Eff you, too, chapters! And pretty covers! And all things expected of a book!*

I believe this rebellion toward the makeup of a "normal" book stemmed from my approximately 20 minutes of research earlier that week on how to get a book published. I, of course, had no book to publish. I didn't want to waste my precious time writing if there was no chance of publication. And, based on my *extensive* 20 minutes of research, I decided that I was doomed.

The two articles I skimmed said that I needed to write in a specific format and the font needed to be as such and the title should be catchy. All of the sudden, in less time than it takes to cook a frozen pizza, I had gone from being passionate about writing a book to feeling completely deflated.

One article said I needed to have a story that really resonated with people. How the heck am I supposed to know what will and will not resonate with people? In my typical isolating hermit state, I was certain that I was the only human with all of my crazy thoughts and idiosyncrasies and obsession with anthropromorphization, which is a big fancy word I learned once that means I apply human characteristics to inanimate objects. For instance, my car's name is Javier Armando Butler, we have the same initials, and he is a gay Latino man. My stapler has an eyeball sticker on it and his name is Mr. Stapler and we have a very good relationship.

So, since I was clearly the only one in the whole world who did these things, the option of writing something resonant was out. The next option was to have a really cool story. Something profound. Going from a depressive agnostic/atheist workaholic binge-eating addict who believed the only way to success and to writing my book was working an intense corporate job and saving money and then using that money to pay for traveling across Europe because clearly I need external inspiration in the form of things I've never seen before (because taking a weekend trip to the Georgia mountains that I've never seen would be entirely too sensical to inspire me, you see) *to* a sober spiritual open-minded person who uses her intuitive abilities for a living was not *nearly* an exciting enough story. No. It needed to be bigger and better!

Option number three for successful memoir was to already be famous. *Well, shit. How am I gonna' get famous, then?*

All of this inspired the creation and startup of a non-profit organization called SHOCK AWAKE!

I decided that the book should be a traveling book and one that a bunch of strangers would write together, one by one. Each book would begin with 5-10 writing prompts to help people share their anonymous truths. The readers/writers would have the book for a 24-hour period of time, answer everything they could, and then place it in public. Then, some other lucky human would come upon the title-less book and become its next writer.

I loved the idea and was certain that it was brilliant and would take off. And then I'd become famous, of course, and be able to write my memoir about how my communications with a squirrel named Steve changed the face of writing.

As of now, there are twenty-something of those books traveling the world. I know of one that has made it to Ireland. I wanted (and still want) thousands of these books in circulation. I think it's an excellent and safe and interesting outlet for people's brain gerbils and emotional baggage. Perhaps, in time, there will be thousands. Perhaps not.

Some of the written prompts are really deep and vulnerable and intense. I told my friend, Acrobat, about the book idea. (He's an actor who climbs unclimbable things and can break dance and do backflips, hence his name for this book.)

"Do you really think the world is ready for that?" He asked.

"Is the world ready for uninhibited and anonymous honesty? You freaking bet. We *need* it. This is past due!" I responded.

Rather than merely hand-write a few handfuls of books and put them out into the world, I went full-out and created a fancy website and applied for 501(c)3 status. I applied in February of 2015. I now have the finalized paperwork in my office with the attached request for an $800ish check to finalize this status. Yea, sure, IRS. I'll get right to that. I have roughly $7 in my bank account (I deposited $5 cash yesterday). Can I put it on layaway?

The website to the non-profit organization is www.shockawake.org, by the way, if it still exists when you read this. I hope it does. I've known for a while that I am here to help shock the world awake with uninhibited truth and unabashed honesty and other combinations of words that mean the same thing. Perhaps this will occur via those books. Maybe it'll be via this one that you're holding. Or maybe it's C. All of the above.

Now here I am, a year and a half after the inspirational squirrel chat, writing a book with no format, no headings or chapter things, no page numbers, and no title. Although this may have changed in between my writing it and you holding it, messy stream-of-consciousness is what brought the book to life. Maybe twenty-something people will buy and read this one. Maybe not. Frankly, it's none of my business. My duty is to write.

~ * ~

I was explaining this book to someone recently and said:

"It's non-fiction. It's the most authentic writing I've ever done. I am writing whatever feels right at any given moment. Sometimes it's journal entries, sometimes it's rambling, sometimes it's like standup comedy. There's heartbreak and heartache and humor and wit and random concerns. There's addiction and recovery and bouts of wisdom and doodles. Pretty much, it's me. It's me as a book."

I gave that explanation to a lovely Publix cashier named David and he acted legitimately amped about reading it. I told him I'd be done within a week and published in a month. It came out of my mouth without me thinking about it. It's either wishful thinking or the book showing its confidence. I don't even know if it's possible to publish a book in such a short period of time. I promised him I'd bring him a copy. He said he's working there for the next four months, so I've got a *little* bit of padding.

While taking Floyd on a soul walk today (where he and I walk the neighborhood without a cell phone and I focus on things I'm grateful for and concentrate on feeling as if my dreams have already come true), I focused on what it will feel like to be a NY Times best-selling author. I imagined my mailbox overflowing with letters from people who related to my words and felt inspired or helped in some way. I imagined having a six-month window to write my next book.

I felt my stride change. I felt a weight lift off of my shoulders. I felt a sensation of *I made it. I did it.* THEN I realized two big things:

1. I'm still me. Even when my book is published and people read it, I'll still have my emotions and idiosyncrasies and likely still have my obsession with almond butter.
2. The pressure I felt lift off of my shoulders *doesn't actually exist.* That is pressure I put onto myself and it doesn't do anyone any good. I can release it at any time.

C. Might as well throw a third realization in there: Acting "as if" helps to build neural pathways which are in support of my goals rather than re-enforcing old behavior. Granted, I totally get hung up on how far to take this. For instance, if a cashier at Publix asks me when my book will be out (hypothetically speaking), do I act *as if* it'll be out in a month and tell him as such? *Or is that lying?* Ouch, my brain.

One thing is for certain: as soon as I shifted into feeling how it will feel to have a published book, I was propelled into action. I guess I have to actually write a book in order to get one published. Funny how that works.

~ * ~

Around the time of the session with Mentor in October 2014, I was spending 8-12 hours each day on self-discovery and recovery work. I had also begun the twelve-week course of The Artist's Way. I would wake up by 5:30am, no matter what time I went to bed (adjusting the alarm according to the aforementioned circadian sleep cycle as learned from The Owner's Manual to the Brain) to write my Morning Pages for thirty minutes, meditate for 45 minutes to an hour, exercise, write my daily affirmations, and eat a Breakfast of Kings, as I called it. I would then shower and dive into my weekly work for The Artist's Way as well as whatever other spiritual book I was reading at the time. I highlighted, wrote in the margins of books, and took notes. My workaholism had found a new home via my spiritual awakening.

I focused heavily on how to increase my intuitive abilities. I wanted to communicate with the spiritual realm. I wanted to see my spirit guides and physically see ghosts. However, I was still incredibly afraid of the dark (I had been since I was a kid). Clairsentience was one of my strongest abilities at first, where I could physically and emotionally feel energetic presences which I could not yet see. This was hard for me to grasp, what with a history of drug use and diagnosed mental disorders and the corresponding hallucinations of prescribed medications. It was difficult for me to let go of the label of "crazy" when referring to believing in something I couldn't physically see.

The way I look at it now, thankfully, is this: Love is not something that can be seen, but it can be felt. Walking into a room where there's tension is something that is felt but not seen. The connection between two cell phones clearly exists, though it's not something that laymen can explain or that human folk can see with their physical eyes. We spend much of our lives believing in things we cannot see, yet the concept of earthbound spirits and other out-there stuff oftentimes coincides with a label of fake or crazy. I think this ties into fear. I believe people would rather *not* believe in any of this stuff. I mean, coming to the realization that there is way more to life than what meets the eye has been pretty terrifying for me. It's also been rather invigorating.

I learned through my extensive research that the energetic presences I felt were earthbound spirits. The type of spirits I attracted at that period in my life were low-vibrating and warped and were victims of homicide or suicide or some other sudden deaths. They weren't the kindest people. I've since realized that, just like the living, these folks normally just wanted to be heard. At the core of their behavior and behind their outer appearances was typically a wounded and traumatized child.

I read about creating energetic boundaries—something else that couldn't be physically seen—yet I was hesitant to do anything about it. When I was younger and watched movies like The Sixth Sense, I remember feeling jealous of the characters who could speak with ghosts. I wanted to have that ability. I wanted to be special. Then, upon finding out that I do have that ability (as does everyone), I didn't want to get rid of it or scare the ghosties away!

As such, I attracted more.

As such, my energy drained. I began dealing with attachments, which was scary. I'd go from being happy spiritual Jen to feeling an energetic presence to all of the sudden ripping stuff off of my walls and feeling intense anger for no apparent reason. Again, Inner Critic told me I was insane. But, with help from Mentor and automatic writing and research, I learned that these were spirits "jumping" my body. Apparently 75% of people have some sort of spiritual attachment. That was a daunting statistic for me to read.

I was soon informed that these lower-vibrating entities fed off of fear and negativity. As I felt afraid, I attracted them even more. One day, I decided to be brave and walk *toward* an energetic entity in my apartment rather than scurrying and hiding like I normally did.

"I am not afraid of you. Get out of my apartment." I said while walking through the area of my apartment where I felt the presence.

This. Was. Terrifying. Yet, I survived. And the presence left. I continued to do this until I finally realized that these people were in *my* space. I am denser than they are. I am alive and, when they're in my space, I am now willing to tell them to leave. I said it gently at first, but there were some folks with whom I had to be rather straight-forward. This is a lifetime of building boundaries with the living, too, so this process has been an excellent learning experience for me.

Additionally, this is the same approach I use with other types of fear. Fear of writing this book, for instance, is being surpassed by my walking *toward* it and continuing to write. While I do believe there is a time and place to listen to fear, I have learned the difference between when something is legitimately dangerous versus when my old programming is trying to keep me in a little box of safety.

Come to find out, discomfort is a good thing. It means that we're growing. Right now, as I write this, I am severely uncomfortable. Thankfully, I am utilizing the energy to express myself rather than hide from the discomfort. But, just as with building any muscle, repetitive action is key.

~ * ~

One of the hardest parts of my awakening has been around the topic of food. This is a multi-faceted topic for me, so I will first focus on how it relates to my sensitivities expanding. My growing sensitivity (as a result of my sobriety and my awakening) made it difficult to go into public for many months. I would pick up on things from other people that I had no other way of knowing. Standing in line in Starbucks, for instance, I'd become inundated with thoughts and emotions that weren't mine.

This also happened when I ate meat. While eating chicken, I'd suddenly feel scared, panicky, and have morbid images of what I can only assume were what the chicken saw last. The same thing happened with cows. I dealt with a lot of anger and fear and feelings of claustrophobia. I finally realized that, since everything is energy, my consuming the animal meat was me consuming the energy of those animals. This is when I became a vegetarian, which soon turned into veganism. Initially it was hard for my logical brain to believe this as truth, but after so many experiences, I adopted it as *my* truth and made necessary adjustments.

What's more is that I was having reactions to other foods as well. I had cut gluten after reading the fabulous book Grain Brain months prior (and having discovered through keeping a food journal that I reacted poorly to gluten), but I suddenly became hypersensitive to food that had even *touched* gluten. The same thing happened with tomatoes, peanut butter, and many others. I continued cutting foods until I was down to the very bare minimum.

One of the other aspects of food has been an unhealthy relationship with it in regards to my body image. There was one point in my life when I was active in my addiction that I ate a brownie fudge sundae every day. This went on for about a month. I'd also polish off a box of cereal while sitting on my kitchen floor, all the while feeling guilty for eating so much. I remember regularly thinking and saying aloud "I wish I was allergic to all unhealthy foods. Then I'd stay skinny." Well, this is sort of what happened. (Our words are our prayers. Seriously.)

As my vibration increased, I needed higher-vibrating fuel for my body and brain. As such, I did end up cutting all of the unhealthy foods and instead focusing on eating an organic, vegan diet of mostly raw foods.

This went well at first, but I found myself getting sick a few months in. I was lethargic and exhausted and sometimes even struggling more with depression and the yearning to hermit. I mostly felt zapped of energy and drive. I mean, I got *really* extreme and strict with my diet. Thankfully, I talked with a manager of a local vitamin shop about it. I was taking 17 types of supplements per day, I told him, and eating a raw, organic, vegan diet… Yet I still felt awful.

That's when he recommended the blood type book, Eat Right 4 Your Type. He explained that some foods are medicine to my blood type and some are poison.

I discovered that my blood type was B+, which I found hilarious because "Be Positive!" has been a repeating theme in my life. I went to Barnes & Noble and read the book. It made so much sense. I started to add foods back in as they correlated with my blood type and I started to feel better. I added meat back in, ensuring it was free range and grass fed and organic, and I also started blessing all of my food. My intense bloating and itching stopped. My skin cleared up a bit. And, most excitingly, I had energy again. This was such a lovely turning point for me.

While I don't think the blood type diet has *all* of the answers or that there is necessarily a "right" way to eat, I know that it has worked wonders for me. Over the years, I've kept track of my eating and my emotional and physical reaction to the fuel I choose. This has been empowering. I now know which foods do and do not mix well with my body and can plan and act accordingly. Now, when I deal with a physical discomfort, I'm able to tune into my body and discover its origin. Is it because of something I ate? Is it an emotion I'm digesting rather than expressing? Is it dehydration and exhaustion? By treating myself

one theory { GOD food vs. Man food

like my own adorable research project, I've become pretty fluent on how the vehicle of Jen runs.

~ * ~

Today, I was called to write down all of the fears I could think of. From there, I dissected the fears. *Why am I afraid of this?* Through this dissection process, I came down to three basic fears recurring throughout my life with different masks: fear of failure, fear of self, and fear of dying alone. Honestly, I had no idea that these were fears of mine. Fear of failure is intertwined all throughout my life. There are so many things I unknowingly have been interpreting as failure.

I've known since I was a kid that I was here for great things. I believe we are *all* here for great things, and I also believe that in some people's soul contract in a specific lifetime, there's some big stuff on the agenda. And, since I've been preparing for this lifetime for a long time and this is my soul's last hoorah here on this planet *and* since I'm sort of a GO BIG OR GO HOME kind of person at heart, I am certain that this lifetime stands to be a powerful one.

For a long time, I thought I was using this as motivation. Upon working on my list of fears this morning, though, I realized that I've been using it as a spikey form of "DO IT OR ELSE" pressure.

Here's the thing. We all affect others. As I move through my day, interacting with people face-to-face or via my cell phone or someone reading an article I've written, I am impacting others. Those people, in turn, interact with other people, further spreading the energy I've given to them. It works the other way, too. This is why it is extremely important to remain in a state of kindness toward others. We are constantly affecting our surroundings, whether we realize it or not.

So, as much as I desire to share the messages gifted to me via writing and as hellbent as I am on becoming a NY Times best-selling author, the fear of failure is silly-talk. Even if my writing doesn't get into the hands of millions of people, that doesn't mean I've failed at helping to raise the vibration of the earth. Each and every day that I live in gratitude and in the present moment, I am helping the collective consciousness do the same.

If you go out and make an effort to genuinely smile at ten people, you are assisting in increasing your *and* their joy. Additionally, the ripple effect of your genuine smile stands to continue onward and outward. A seemingly simple smile or compliment or kind gesture stands to make a drastic improvement in someone's day, or many people's days.

Rather than take this as pressure, I think it's important to take this as fact. Use it as motivation. This has personally helped me to treat others in a way I'd want to be treated, no matter how angry or rude they may be. I know one thing is for sure; when I was an angry and mean person, I was also miserable and in pain. One of my favorite sayings that I've heard recently is that *hurt people hurt people.* When keeping this in mind, it becomes easier to have kindness and compassion as a regular state of being.

Something big for me has been removing my attachment to outcomes. For instance, I used to hold doors open for lots of people, but then simultaneously have growing amounts of resentment for each person who neglected to tell me thank you. I'd obnoxiously go "YOU'RE WWEELLCCOOMMMEEE" as they walked away. So really, when the mask is removed and I look more deeply into my motivation, I see that my door-opening was more of my seeking approval and acknowledgements than it was helping others. This has happened a lot throughout my life.

Now that I'm aware of this tendency, I regularly enjoy kicking it in the shins by being kind *even if people are jackasses in return.* Realistically, I haven't a clue what other people are going through. Reminding myself that their reaction has nothing to do with me and that everyone else's life doesn't revolve around me has been *huge* in:

-Humbling myself.

-Letting go of outcomes around my actions.

-Being kind, no matter what.

-Laughing inside at reactions rather than getting my feelings hurt.

-Having good motives behind my actions.

-Realizing that I am not the only person in the whole world. (See: Humbling myself.)

Intention is everything. For a long time, for instance, I donated money *because I read somewhere that donating money would bring ME more money.* That is self-seeking and controlling and not at all what it's supposed to be about. My current understanding around donation is to focus on our true abundance in the present moment. No matter where I stand financially or how much debt I may have or which bills are due tomorrow, I have enough to be alive and present *right now.* I have enough to be breathing and taking in the bountiful view of this earth.

~ * ~

Did you know that there are colors in nature? I swear, before I quit drinking and then quit taking anti-depressants, I saw life in black and white. Or, at the very least, I viewed it through a dulled lens or old, dirty glasses. Today, I went for a walk with my dad. For *years* I held onto this victim mentality because my dad didn't invite me to hang out with him more. Then I suddenly had this idea of *me* inviting *him* to do something. So, I did. And we walked. Without cell phones.

"Is it hard getting old?" ← My first question. What? I'm brutally honest. Pops and I don't use tact.

"Not really. I enjoy it. Because I have an entire lifetime of knowledge and experiences. I feel like I'm at the top, looking down."

"I'm liking myself the older I get, too. Because even my f*ck-ups have brought me to where I am."

"I don't see anything as a f*ck-up. Because realistically, in the moment, things probably seemed like good ideas. Sure, drinking tequila and jumping off of a rooftop may not have been a good idea in hindsight, but in the moment it was a *great* idea. So I can look back and recognize that I've done the best I could at any given time. Then there are no regrets."

Such wisdom from this lovely man with his tube socks and khaki shorts.

We walked about a quarter mile to the neighborhood lake, where he faked out a couple of ducks and geese and a swan by pretending to have food when he had none. He found this hilarious. And then we gently debated about whether or not the geese were geese. He said they were mallards. They weren't. They were geese.

I digress.

While walking back, I stopped and gasped and pointed.

"Do you see that purple on that tree?" I asked.

"Yes. Beautiful." Dad responded.

"I didn't even know that existed! In real life!"

"Yep. Good stuff."

We continued walking.

"*And this grass!*" I dramatically exclaimed, "It's the most vibrant shade of green in the whole wide world!"

"Very pretty," he said.

In those moments, while focusing on my current surroundings, I was free of concern about tomorrow. I wasn't worrying about student loan interest piling up over the years or wondering about whether or not this book will be published. No. I was present, man. Fully present. And life, in that very moment, was *more* than enough.

Life, in every moment, is *more* than enough. It's all about how I choose to perceive it. Those vibrant colors are always available to me. Taking a walk with a friend or a family member is an option available to me every day. Focusing on what I do have rather than what I don't have is a powerful vibration to put out into the Universe. Also, it is a *way* less stressful way to live.

Gratefullness makes what we have... enough.

~ * ~

Throughout the years, Chance visited me in my dreams often, normally as a chestnut. One time, he showed himself as a unicorn and pranced around in all his mystical glory. A few months after my twenty-eighth birthday, he again came to me in a dream. This time, though, he had a very clear message. He told me that he had reincarnated as a dog. He showed me a brief image of a puppy. Chance said the puppy was a male, eight weeks old, and was at Petsmart. He proudly reiterated the color of the puppy: chestnut.

I had no previous intentions of getting a dog and felt a bit of skepticism around the dream's message, so I asked for a sign from the Universe. I had an image flash into my head of this puppy being the only one left. I was in the worst financial situation of my life since I had quit my corporate job six months prior, so I said aloud, "Chance, if it is you, get your price lowered."

Actor and I drove to Petsmart the next day. It was windy and chilly outside and there was one makeshift gated cage remaining. I walked up to the cage and stared down at a chunky, wrinkly, chestnut puppy. Next to him was a chunky, wrinkly, black puppy.

Not the only one left, I thought. *Oh well.*

Before my thought had finished, a couple walked up to the cage, bent over, and scooped up the black puppy.

"That one's yours," the woman said with a smile.

I looked down at the wrinkly-faced chestnut puppy. He was the only puppy left (of 23 that had been there, I later learned). I read the information on the outside of the gate: Lab/Boxer mix, male, 8 weeks old.

My left brain kept trying to tell me different logical explanations for all of this. *Orange dogs are common… So are puppies around this age. You came toward the end of the day; of COURSE there is only one left.*

"Babe! Did you just hear that man?!" Actor pointed to a man with two sons who had just passed us. I shook my head no.

"That man just said, 'Let's go, Chance. CHANCE! Come on!'" Apparently, one of the sons was named Chance. Actor and I both got chills. Immediately afterward, the owner of the adoption foundation offered to lower the price $50.

I then proceeded to pay for a puppy with a credit card.

The puppy's name is Floyd and he wears a pink collar. (Pink + Floyd. Get it? He's a walking pun.) He plays tag with me. He curls up next to me while I read. He nips at my butt to get a laugh. He always seems to know exactly what is needed to set my mind at ease. When I am sad, he walks up to me, places his paws on my chest, and puts his snout on my shoulder, as if hugging me. I hug him back, knowing I have reconnected with a long lost friend.

The void that I had felt since Chance died has been filled. Sometimes, I accidentally call Floyd "Chance." His favorite treats are carrots and he regularly rears and rolls just like a horse. It's rather amazing to watch.

This experience is what really sparked my belief in animal communication *and* in reincarnation. It also helped me to begin trusting my intuitive guidance.

~ * ~

Expression is a form of release and also a form of replenishment. It transmutes and dispels the old, making room for new shiny things to come in.

I am feeling stressed about this book because I don't know what it is. I don't remember everything I've written and I fear that I am going all over the place and won't be able to tame it enough to make it publishable. Perhaps that's the point. Perhaps the point is for it to be chaotic and messy and real, even though I lately have been wondering if this book has been my memoir's way of getting itself out of me and onto paper. By changing shapes.

I've a shape-shifting memoir.

Hm. I like that.

Zuck. I don't know if this book is about depression and suicidality or if it's about my spiritual awakening. And I—Okay. The answer just came to me which was

It's about YOU. So ALL OF THE ABOVE.

GAH. This is difficult.

No, it isn't. You're attempting to make it difficult in an effort to prevent yourself from moving forward. Stop trying to make this book any certain way. The only definitions you have for "normal" books are ones you've read or experienced in the past. Allow this to be what it is. Allow it to shape-shift and morph and flow. Allow yourself to do the same. It isn't about being correct or organized or XYZ enough. It isn't about being in order. It's about being true to you. It is about authentic expression. And it is about moving through resistance and conquering a goal you've had in place essentially since birth.

You are a writer. You are here to help change the face of how books are written. It matters not what the editing process looks like. You're not ready to edit yet. Your awareness is not yet there. The flow state is with your writing now and, once you've finished writing, the flow state will broaden to also encompass editing. So breathe. Rest easy into the present moment. Realize that whatever way the words come out of you is the correct way for them to come out. Be messy. Be real. Be you.

Wow. Okay. Fine.

I guess, when it comes down to it, these words are the embodiment of my dream coming to fruition. Having a "first book" is a scary step, but it is the completion of this goal that will help my second and third books feel easier. By book number ten, I'll be a pro.

The lesson that I'm choosing to take from this back-and-forth inner dialogue is that creativity needn't a definition or even a genre… *Especially* during the creative process. I believe that this book is showing itself to me. It's almost as though I'm starting with a big hunk of stone and allowing a sculpture to present itself to me. Rather than waste time wondering what it will be, I choose to trust and continue chipping away.

~ * ~

I decided to make 2015 my last year taking medication. I had already stopped taking Goodies powder and Midol and Gas-X and all of the other drugs I used to regularly consume. By this time, I was taking my prescribed dosage of Adderall and Wellbutrin for ADHD and depression, respectively. However, I was dedicating my life to embracing my sensitivities and I felt that medication was preventing me from fully accessing them. For me, it felt right to quit.

Honestly, I felt sort of hypocritical while taking meds. I ate such healthy food and was an energy healer and had done so much work on releasing past life trauma and emotional trauma held in my body. I meditated regularly and was living a sober lifestyle. Taking medication felt inauthentic. It felt out-of-alignment.

It also felt necessary. I was admittedly terrified to quit taking these prescriptions. I had experienced life without medication before. Sure, it had been *before* sobriety and before the amount of personal work I'd done, but there was only one aspect that stuck out to me: suicide. I deeply feared that my yearning to die would bubble back up… And I would give into the intense feeling. I feared I'd lose myself. Truly, in hindsight, I feared *myself.*

And it makes sense, right? If I lived full-time with a person who was constantly kicking me while I was down, saying horribly mean things about my body and my mind, telling me I'd be better off dead, and actually attempting to kill me, it'd take a substantial amount of time before I'd consider trusting that person again.

Anti-depressants felt like a shield from myself. I worried that, without them, I'd fall off of the deep end. And, although my prior two psych ward hospitalizations didn't teach me much, it was during those visits that I learned (from other patients) the *right* and *best* ways to successfully commit suicide. This is knowledge I wished I hadn't absorbed.

I informed my psychiatrist of my desire to lower and ultimately get off of medication. He was supportive, although also seemingly skeptical.

Sure, my past experiences *off* of medication didn't yield much hope for my future. However, I felt confident that I would one day live an emotionally stable life, free of medication. That is how I started the journey, actually, was repeating that phrase to myself. "I am emotionally stable, free of medication."

I once had a convincing conversation with a gypsy girl who wore handmade clothes, during which she explained that the Universe doesn't understand "no." So, by saying "I do not want to take medication," I am actually saying, "I do want to take medication." I remember, at the time, I told her "I never want to work for a corporation again."

Her response was, "I bet you're getting a lot of corporate offers; aren't you?"

I made a scrunch face at her and nodded. *How the heck did she know that?*

"That's because you're asking the Universe to send you the jobs."

"No. I said that I never want to work for another person again. I *don't* want it."

"The Universe is free of judgment. It overlooks 'no' and 'never' and anything negative in nature."

"So," I began to understand, "I am saying that I want to work for another person again."

"Yes."

"But I don't want to! I mean, I'd rather no—AH. How do I word it?"

"Word it positively."

"I work for myself and I love what I do?"

"Perfect. How does that feel?"

It felt good. *Really* good. I have since made a [consistent, recurring] effort to adopt this way of speaking. It can be difficult at times. However, in my repeated affirmations and during prayers, I make super-duper extra sure that negatives are left elsewhere.

Rather than saying, "I don't want to take medication anymore" Or "I no longer take medication," I shifted to "I am emotionally stable and free of medication." I wrote this multiple times. When I took my morning dosage of Wellbutrin and Adderall, I'd hold them both in my hands and say aloud, to what/whomever was listening, "Please help me withdraw off of these medications."

~ * ~

By this time of my life, I *had* recognized a power greater than myself. I called it Universe or Spirit. Sometimes I'd call it the Nonlocal Intelligence per one of Deepak Chopra's books. I had watched The Secret and begun learning about Law of Attraction and how to utilize it for my benefit. (For those unfamiliar, the basic premise is that the Universe responds to emotion. So, if I want to have a book published, my choosing to *feel that it already is published* is attracting that reality toward me. Do some research, should you so desire. It's fascinatingly powerful.)

I remember the first time watching The Secret. It was even before my spiritual awakening. I decided to focus on manifesting the presence of a blue bird. I was told to try something simple like a free cup of coffee or a phone call from a friend. I chose a blue bird. That is what I wanted to bring to fruition in my life. I imagined the blue bird and I imagined how I'd feel upon seeing the blue bird. Within five minutes, I gave up and called The Secret crap. (This was such a tendency of mine. Without immediate proof of something giving me what I wanted, I'd oftentimes quit shortly after starting.) Then, while driving, I saw something in the road. As I quickly approached it, I saw what it was. *It was a blue bird. And it wasn't moving.*

Before I could even stop the car, I hit the blue bird. It is the only time I have ever hit an animal while in my car. I remember screaming and feeling a *lot* of emotions. I drove home immediately and cried, coming up with a story of multiple blue birds having attempted to get my attention, only I had been too up my own ass to recognize them. So this one brave bird, I decided, had sacrificed himself to bring my wish to life.

I'd realized that it worked, this Law of Attraction stuff. And, in learning more about it, I began utilizing affirmations and Law of Attraction meditations even more. While I do know of the Law of Attraction as a factual part of our existence in this realm, I also know that I utilized it to play God. I started manifesting things in life and experiencing more and more synchronicities. This part was (and is) great. My issue was that, since thoughts are prayers, I was frequently [unknowingly] praying for more difficulty to come my way based on my own internal dialogue.

See, my good moods were always contingent upon something. If I got a client, I was in a good mood. If I fit into my skinny jeans, I was in a good mood. If Actor and I were doing well, I was in a good mood. When things were *not* going according to my plan, however, is when I'd slip into self-pity mode. It was as though I was doing all of the self-healing acts with *attached expectation*. I was essentially saying, "Hey. Universe. Here's the game plan. Ima' do XYZ and then I'm gonna' need you to make my life look like THIS."

Here's something else that's coming to light right now. I think, to an extent, the above approach works. Me ordering something from the Universe totally works. However, it may be one heck of a journey to get to a place of receiving what I've ordered. The journey's bumpy ride may look and feel *nothing* like what we *think* it ought to look like. This is where trust comes into play.

For instance, I have been asking and at times demanding that I have a book published before my thirtieth birthday. As of now, the chances are still good for this to happen. Before this current flow-state of writing? I unsuccessfully started roughly a dozen books. I had to go through a rather intense heartbreak, be forced to really look at and take inventory of myself, and eat many slices of humble pie in order to be in my current mental state of allowance. During those rough bouts, my present-moment life didn't seem to at all line up with writing and publishing a piece of work. I mostly felt way off track and as though I was taking steps backward rather than forward.

What I am saying is this: what if our dreams and prayers *are* coming true? What if every single moment, no matter how painful or uncomfortable or unplanned or seemingly off-course, is a moment closer to these dreams coming to fruition? We don't get to choose what the dream-fulfilling process looks like. If we do choose what it looks like, we are limiting ourselves to our conscious human knowledge which, no matter how smart we are, is inadequate in comparison to our souls… Or to the Universe.

I still struggle to relinquish control. I have found that the process of surrender is a cyclical one that looks like this:

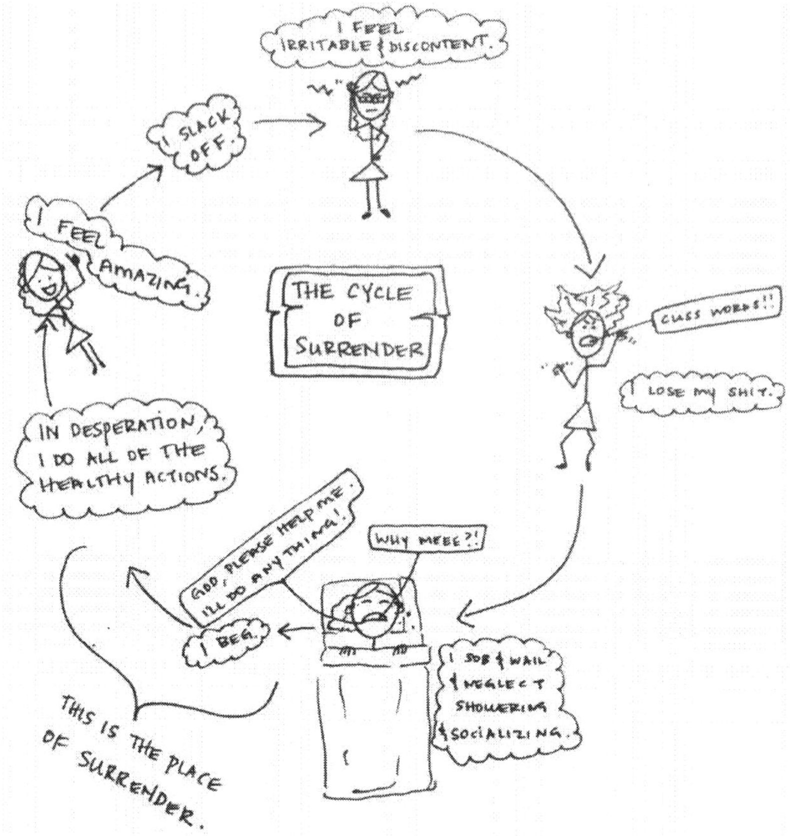

~ * ~

Actor and I moved in together into a beautiful 2,000 square foot home with a fenced-in backyard and a two-car garage and, of course, a bouncy puppy named Floyd. I was certain Actor was it. "The one" and all of that. I loved how much he felt. I loved that he introduced me to sage and to certain music. I loved that we made up ridiculous songs and danced to Miley Cyrus in his incredibly messy Nissan Sentra, Alan.

He helped me become less rigid. He also helped me become rather good at Call of Duty: Black Ops. I see this as quite an accomplishment, since the thought of sitting still long enough to play videogames or watch a television show brought much anxiety ever since I'd adopted sobriety. There was this constant feeling of "GAAAH! I should be DOING something rather than wasting away on a sofa!" Relaxation was not my specialty.

It still isn't.

I digress.

I loved the romantic idea of me winning an Oscar for writing a movie and him winning one for acting in it. I frequently envisioned us in our high-rise apartment in New York and the other details of what it would be like when we were rich and famous. He was (and is) a phenomenal actor.

When we first moved into the house, the energy upstairs was, as my loving Mommy would say, *yucky poo kaka*. The best way I can describe it is that it felt thick, murky, sticky, and draining. I know that the previous inhabitants left abruptly after having not paid rent for three months. The energetic imprint of anxiety in the upstairs bedroom was impossible to ignore. Because of this, Actor and I created a floor bed on the first floor near the fireplace. It was fun… Almost like our own little fort. Floyd slept with us, too. I put crystals and salt in the upstairs rooms and regularly burned sage in them.

The imprint of the house still affected us. We found ourselves both feeling unconfident about the relationship, seemingly out of nowhere. There was tension that neither of us understood or could explain. It wasn't until a random Starbucks (Or, as Actor called it, StarBoodles) visit that we began to piece it all together. After sitting at Boodles for about thirty minutes, him sipping on his grande black iced coffee and me on my tall iced decaf Americano, we made eye contact. The tension had been released and the spark showed itself to us again. We hugged and said hi to each other, as if we hadn't seen one another in a month. In a sense, I don't think we had. I am not completely certain how it all works, but I believe he and I had fallen into the energetic imprint left by the previous couple. (I also recognize that there's a period of adaptation when first moving in together. However, having lived with people before, I am able to recognize the difference between that type of behavior and what Actor and I experienced.) We vowed to clean and clear and bless the place.

We spent an entire evening doing it. I played Tibetan chanting music while we physically cleaned. Afterward, we saged and used salt and said prayers to bless the entire house. Lastly, we put our clothes in the washing machine and nakedly scurried upstairs to take a clearing salt bath. The relief was palpable. If you've never cleared your house, I deeply recommend that you do so.

There was still a little tension, but we began settling in nicely and recognizing which were our feelings versus the past inhabitants'. I saged and cleared the house regularly, playing good music and dancing around in an effort to put a more positive energetic imprint into the house.

One night, while lying in the floor bed, I reached out and touched Actor's back. I loved nuzzling him, but, since I felt a stand-offish feeling coming from him, I kept my space, reached out, and touched him. He jerked away. I touched him again.

"Are you okay?" I asked.

"Just-DON'T TOUCH ME. Okay?!" He responded.

I backed off. He'd never spoken to me in such a way. He remained silent. I copied the approach for as long as I could, staring at the raised ceiling.

I remember I had done my first hypnotherapy appointment that day, and the primary focus was on authentically expressing and *actually feeling* my emotions and concerns and truth rather than codependently holding them in. This gave me a sense of courage to communicate rather than maintain silence.

"Are you okay? What is going on with you?" I finally asked, with my gentlest tone possible. "Seriously. Please be honest with me."

He divulged a handful of things. He said he didn't like when I touched him. Not when I massaged him, not when I scratched his back, not when I played with his hair, not when I snuggled him while sleeping. (This was tough to swallow after nearly a year of regularly doing all of the above.) After more digging on my part, he went on to explain that he found me controlling and manipulative. He also said I acted like I was better than him. He felt like he had to be on his best behavior all of the time.

In the moment? I was floored. Now? I get it. I really do.

I wish I could say that I've completely healed from codependency and manipulative (or "jenipulative," as I call it) tendencies. I have done a lot of work in that regard (through Al-Anon, reading books on codependency, journaling, and severely isolating from all humans because then THERE'S NO WAY TO BE CODEPENDENT, RIGHT?! Ahem.), and new layers regularly are exposed to me. I'll think that I have it all figured out, and then suddenly a friend will fall away, I'll have a minor breakdown, and ultimately realize, *Oh shit. I was being uber codependent and leechy with that person. Dangit.* ← That's an example of a slice of humble pie.

The relationship with Actor fell away and he moved out. We remain friends to this day. I feel extreme fondness toward him and it is my understanding that he feels similarly toward me. The relationship was an opportunity for me to learn lots of lessons. I learned that, even if I do everything "right," life will still happen in its own way. I made such an effort to be the most supportive, the most honest, the most loyal, the most accommodating, and the most everything… Except for the most Jen. That's what I was unknowingly avoiding. And, realistically, that's all that either of us needed to do to have kept our bond alive. Was to be uninhibitedly ourselves. However, we simply weren't ready. It took me losing something like our beautiful connection in order for me to *really* take a look at some of my deep-rooted relationship patterns.

Come to find out, even though I did *all* of the nice actions (such as laundry, cleaning, present-buying, back-scratches, videogame-playing, etc.), they were all done with an attached expectation. I was acting this way in an effort to be the best girlfriend for him. I also was admittedly acting this way in an effort to get him to be the best boyfriend for me. This explains why he felt pressured to be on his best behavior, because that expectation truly did exist.

I've recognized this unhealthy tendency to love people for their potential rather than for where they are now—myself included. This apparently can make a relationship with me rather exhausting. I am now to a place in life where I'm beginning to instead fall in love with imperfections. Quirks. Moments of nonsensical emotional basketcasery. Lapses in rationality. All of it. When people share their messy humanness with me, I feel bucking honored. What's even more exciting is that I'm able to do that for myself. Once I started really holding space for myself, being patient and holding space for others became second nature.

This wasn't something within my awareness during my time with Actor. Back then, it was easier to point the finger at him and his actions without taking into account my own. Thankfully, I'm able to look back fondly and with gratitude and apply what I've learned to my *current* friendships (and eventual relationships). I know that I did the best I could from where I was, mentally and emotionally. I know the same holds true for Actor. This is not to say that I haven't experienced intense grief as a reaction to the death of our relationship. I've lost count of the jars of almond butter I've consumed since then. I completely isolated for many months. I also have sort of sworn off relationships because I'm like, *THEY ONLY SEEM REALLY GREAT UNTIL THEY'RE NOT AND BY THEN IT'S TOO LATE AND I WON'T REALIZE UNTIL MANY MOONS LATER THAT I EFFED UP EVEN WHEN I TRIED HARD NOT TO SO WHAT IS THE POINT.*

So. There's an example of where I'm a work in progress. I'm still riding the ol' pendulum, waiting to get flung off onto more stable, well-rounded ground.

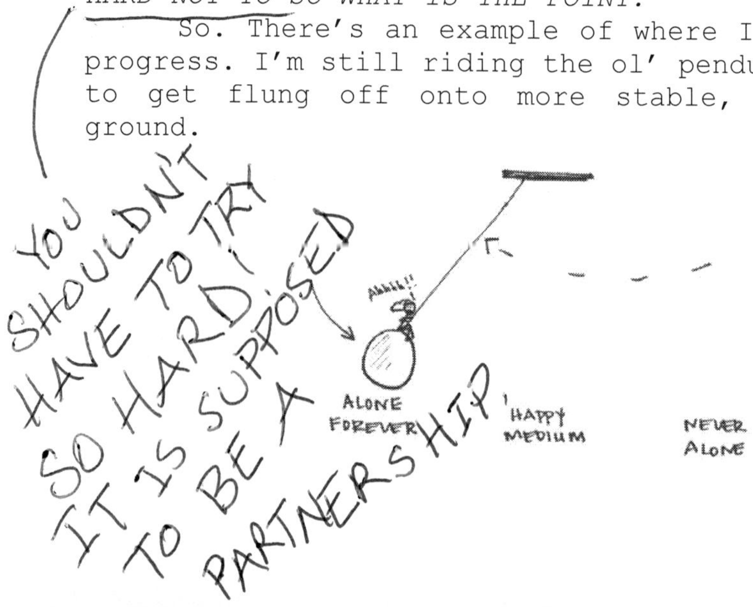
YOU SHOULDN'T HAVE TO TRY SO HARD, IT IS SUPPOSED TO BE A PARTNERSHIP
AHHH!!
ALONE FOREVER
HAPPY MEDIUM
NEVER ALONE

Having Actor be my first sober heartbreak since I was 15 years old, I experienced a *lot* of pain. Through this pain, I realized how deeply imperative it is to be myself. *That's all I needed to do,* I told myself. *I merely needed to be myself. And he needed to be himself.*

Myself? You mean… The messy insides that I'm not *supposed to talk about?* You mean I'm supposed to set aside the façade of perfection and being put-together and instead be… ::looks around:: *vulnerable?*

That's petrifying. Before and after my relationship with him, I experienced so much shame about my suicidal ideations and about each new layer of character defects presented to me. I so badly wanted to be perfect first, and *then* share with the world from that place.

So what did I do about that shameful feeling? I shined light on it.

~ * ~

I started writing about my depression, about my suicidality, and about my medication. I did so from a place of self-love rather than lack. Sometimes I was aware and mature about it. Other times, I was messy… Because I felt messy. I wanted to express myself *for* myself and also to reach others who maybe felt similarly.

The posts I shared on social media received amazing feedback. I received private messages from people thanking me for my honesty. They, in turn, shared their stories. This is why I do what I do. I share as openly as I do in an effort to create space for others to share openly, too. Because expression heals. It really freaking does.

I can look back at posts from even a few months ago and pick out bits and pieces as evidence that my victimizing mentality still exists at times. That's okay. Truly, I have become okay with that. Hiding my behind the scenes and waiting to share until I'm 100% ready is an illusory ideal. It's fear's way of keeping me stagnant, stuck, and chasing my tail.

I was regularly posting to my blog in a more vulnerable and raw nature than I'd ever done before. It was invigorating and simultaneously terrifying. Expressing authentically and not having my world suddenly implode as a result began building a foundation of comfort. This wasn't the comfort I'd built upon Actor's back. This wasn't the comfort I'd build from my titles of Reiki Master or Animal Communicator. This was true comfort from my depths, all as a result of being authentic to *me.*

Suddenly, I had an interest in getting out of the house. I decided to search for a scheduled reason to leave and interact with fellow earthlings. You know, that thing called a "job." I discovered a small metaphysical bookstore a few miles from my house and found out that they were hiring for one day a week. *How perfect!* A week later, I met with the owner for an interview. I showed up as Professional Jen, who is one of my more-practiced roles. I was confident. I was maybe even a little cocky.

"I'm gonna' cut to the chase," she said.

"Please. Go right ahead."

"I looked at your website."

"Oh wow! Thanks!"

"And I read your most recent blog…" She trailed off, as if I was supposed to catch her drift.

"Awesome," I said.

"There are some things that concern me," she said. She waved a paper in front of her. On this paper, come to find out, she had written excerpts from my blog entry. The post she was referring to was about my recent bout of darkness and its corresponding emotional releases. I also had written about my prior tendency to obsess myself over self-help books rather than listen to my own inner voice. Overall, I considered what she had read as one of my happier chunks of text. There had been a couple of cuss words involved, in the spirit of authenticity, but I didn't think those would be a problem.

She started to read the chosen excerpts. My eyes widened. She was reading with an unfamiliar tone, one that I most certainly did not channel into words. My palms clammed up and my shoulders tightened as she read her version of my words.

"What if customers read your blog and saw how depressed you were," she said, "and then came into the store to see you here?"

I said nothing.

"Also," she added, "how can you sell self-help books if you hate them?"

I wanted to stand up and scream my case to her. I wanted to flip the table and ninja warrior chop her case of expensive crystals. I wanted to be bitchy to her for bringing my personal life into a business interview and for misconstruing my words in such a way! I wanted to tell her all I'd been through and how unfair she was being.

I wanted to play the comfortable role of victim.

Then, something clicked. I realized that there was no attacker or victim in this situation. My defensiveness was merely an outdated patterned reaction. Also, there was a benefit of her asking me these questions in the way she asked them. This situation had grabbed me from outside of my body and forced me into the present moment. No longer was I Scripted Professional Jen. I became Real Jen.

In this interview, I was given the privilege to share openly and honestly *as myself.* I stumbled at first, explaining to her that some self-help books really *are* shit, but that there are plenty fabulous ones. I told her I had an emotional pendulum swing because I am a human being. All humans experience ups and downs, some of which are really extreme.

"The only difference," I said to her, "is that I'm open and honest about mine."

I cussed. I stammered. I had nothing planned to say, but spoke anyway. I spoke from the heart.

It was terrifying. It was messy. It was *real.*

When I left the interview, I felt raw. I felt exposed. I felt like a baby bird with randomly dispersed feathers poking out of my naked skin.

I never heard back from her. And you know what? I'm grateful. This has allowed me to feel rejection, which I had often avoided. Also, this gave me the privilege of seeing that *real life human beings* are reading my words, which means there are countless interpretations. None of them are wrong. It doesn't matter how spiritual or aware or intuitive I am or how many times I edit a post; I will still inevitably piss someone off. No matter how carefully I craft my words, they will still be digested by unique people with their own trains of experience.

That's kind of liberating, actually.

This removes the self-imposed pressure of writing the "right" thing, which, in my black-and-white thinking, was often my main focus. In actuality, all I need to do is speak from my heart and share it. I don't need to hold the readers' hands. If they come upon my writing, then it is exactly what they need to be reading in that moment. Whether they cry, laugh, growl, do jazz hands, or do nothing in response to my words, there is *something* being worked out inside of them. And frankly, it's none of my business.

I wrote and posted an edited version of the above interview story and submitted it to an online magazine called the elephant journal. *It was accepted for publication*, making it the very first article of mine to be published. A week later, another article was published. That one was entitled "The Real Reason I Think I'm Ugly Today" and was about how I'd begun digging deeper into negative self-talk in an effort to do healing work at a core, inner child level. It was raw and messy. There were cuss words. It was fully authentically me… And an online journal called The Manifest-Station *loved it* and published it, word-for-word.

This is when it really started to sink in for me. This whole approach of authenticity + sharing even when (especially when) feeling really messy apparently was healing for more than just me. *It helped heal others, too.*

It's one of those abstract concepts that is really simple-sounding, yet is incredibly scary to integrate and put into action.

The more I do it? The more in-alignment my life feels. I'm experiencing it more each day that I add to this book. Money shows up when I need it. Friends reach out when I need an ear. Opportunities present themselves seemingly out of nowhere.

This is how I know this God character is a better writer than me. Sure, I always said I'd write a book. I've been saying that since I was newly off of training-wheels on my bicycle. However, I don't know if I ever believed it'd actually happen. And, if I'd written this book in my typically perfectionistic way, it'd have taken me another eleven years to write. The compilation of this book has occurred in a little over *three weeks.* That is outrageous. I never would have assumed such an outcome.

I choose to believe in a higher power because, when I attempt to manage my life, it swiftly becomes a shit-show. When I relax, take it easy, and take action from a place of authenticity and love, life becomes filled with peace and serenity that I never dreamed possible.

~ * ~

In the spirit of staying true to my core and truly experiencing life as Jen, I finally quit taking all medication. In early December 2015, we lowered Wellbutrin (my only remaining prescription) from 200mg/day to 100mg. I experienced a very trying two-week period of time, but I remained gentle and loving with myself. I allowed myself to eat and sleep a little more. There were a few days where I slept 14-

16 hours and still felt exhausted. I look a lot of naps. Some days I was too wiped out to write my positive affirmations or even go for a meditative walk. It didn't matter; I kept going. I kept breathing and sleeping and crying and allowing my body to process and release the medication as well as its corresponding limiting beliefs.

On December 31st, 2015, I took my last dosage of Wellbutrin. I felt nervous, of course, but I also felt supported… By my therapist, my psychiatrist, my friends, and, most importantly (and for the first time ever), I felt fully supported by *myself.*

The process has not been easy. It has been downright difficult. I have been groggy, exhausted, lethargic, sad, and sometimes completely numb. Throughout the process, I ate more, slept more, and worked less. I dealt with anxiety and short bouts of panic. I became even *more* sensitive than I had been prior. Life became even louder than it was.

For example: one night, I watched Lord of the Rings. When the moth communicated with Gandalf on top of that tower thing, I cried. When the orcs were pulling down trees, I cried. When Arwen summoned the power of the river to knock out the bad guys, I cried. When the fellowship made it to Rivendale, I cried. I felt adrenaline during fight scenes, passion during passionate scenes, and anxiety during stressful scenes. Yea, I spent most of the day in bed and had the energy of a 111-year-old hobbit, but I had begun *feeling*.

Many of the days spent detoxing consisted of me wearing the same blue pair of fart-smelling sweatpants and the same mis-matched socks… For days… Without showering. One day, I had a dear friend come over and *bathe me.* That is how "gone" I felt and how little motivation I had.

I refused to give up. I held a knowingness in my heart that each moment of struggle was one step closer to freedom. It was one step closer to actually connecting with that girl in the mirror.

I continued doing my visualizations when I could convince myself to and allowed myself grace when I couldn't. I continued repeating my affirmations, even if I didn't believe them in the moment. I continued to pray and to focus on the energy of gratitude, even when my present moment seemed to encompass nothing but lack. I kept writing every day, even though most of what came out was admittedly crap. It was scattered and oftentimes nonsensical and other times nothing but victimizing brain goo, but I chose not to judge it. I told myself I needed to wade through the crap in order to get to the good stuff.

Eventually, I made it through the extreme sourness. I enjoyed the immense sweetness of the gooey layer of life as I commended myself for having survived the hardest part of withdrawals.

Little did I know, I'd yet to experience the hardest part.

Around Valentine's Day of 2016, I became deeply depressed. I hated to be the stereotypical single girl who was uber depressed on what I consider a silly Hallmark holiday. I've never really applied importance to this specific holiday, but this one left me feeling particularly down. Maybe I was feeling into the collective consciousness of other lonely single women. Who knows?

This was a couple of weeks before my bathtub visit when I learned of all emotions being energy and the importance of removing judgment around emotion. Without this knowledge, I sunk into a tremendous amount of pain and turmoil over my state of being. I fell back into the mindset of something being wrong with me. My tunnel vision returned where suicide seemed like the only way out. Thankfully, though, my awareness had grown enough where I held a glimmer of hope that *these thoughts would not last.* I turned to my writing. Through tears of desperation, I created a list of reasons not to kill myself.

February 14th, 2016

REASONS NOT TO KILL MYSELF:
I'd miss 2016 Olympic gymnastics.
Belly laughs
Naked fight scenes (Viggo Mortenson)
Snuggling with Floyd, my dog
Movie previews

First kisses
Last kisses
Real hugs
Watching a movie for the first time
Dancing when no one is watching
Michael Jackson music
Poor attempts at moonwalking
Organic dark chocolate dipped in almond butter
Mario
Decorating Christmas trees
Snow
Mis-matched socks
Crop-dusting successfully
The feeling of relief after crying
Waking up before the alarm
Eye contact
Dreadlocks
Sea salt baths with candles and essential oils
Massages
Talking in funny accents
Making people laugh
Making a stranger smile
Picking up litter
Board games
When Floyd interrupts me to lick my face
Fires in the fireplace
Crunchy leaves

Thankfully, the list worked. Mostly, I was able to chuckle at myself for some of the reasons. I totally wasn't expecting Viggo Mortenson's naked bod or Olympic gymnastics to help me stay on earth. This exercise helped me shift my focus from the sourness of the present moment to the overall sweetness of my life.

I've realized that the success of this above activity requires more than merely intellectualizing. As in, there is something essential about doing the *action* of writing out a list versus thinking of one. It's all about expression, I've found. Writing these things on paper is almost like placing an order with the Universe. It's a rather powerful exercise. (Get on those naked fight scenes, Viggo.)

On a nerdier level, doing the above list (or something similar) helps to carve out and reinforce new neural pathways rather than staying stuck in the old cycle of suicidality. Overall, it gave me something to *do* with my chaotic inner energy. It helped me survive the moment.

~ * ~

I was hell-bent on logically understanding the existence of a higher power. I had certainly experienced bouts of this connection in the form of synchronicity and other unexplainable circumstances. I felt connected to *some*thing when I was meditating. When talking with fellow spiritual people, I used to term Spirit to describe this higher power simply because that's the term they used.

The closest I got to understanding [what I now call] God from a logical standpoint was reading The Divine Matrix by Gregg Braden. This introduced me to the quantum field of pure potentiality. I also dabbled in Pam Grout's fun and informative books, E Squared and E Cubed, each of which hold nine do-it-yourself experiments to prove that our thoughts really do create our reality. And yes, the experiments work. It was from her books that I snagged the name "Quantum Fred" for whatever this higher power was.

In early 2016, I was called to start a journey: 30 Days of Seeking God. I journaled about it every day and posted a blog entry every day. It was far more transformational (and more difficult) than I had ever anticipated. Overall, it was expansive. It pushed me to a new level of surrender and okayness with not knowing. This thirty-day journey habitually carved out an hour-long period each night that I spent writing, which allowed the transition into writing this book to be a seamless one. I call this synchronistic.

Another synchronicity as a result of this journey was my meeting Publisher, a great dude who owns a local spirituality magazine. About halfway through the thirty days, he and I set up a meeting. And, even though all signs pointed to **YES JEN GO TO THIS**

MEETING, my Inner Saboteur said all sorts of other things to me, such as:

"You probably shouldn't go."

"It won't work out anyway."

"You're in such a bad emotional place right now. You'll probably make a fool of yourself and ruin any chance of a business relationship with this person."

"This is how hard life is always. You should probably give up."

"Crawl back in bed. It's safe there."

I reached out to my closest friend, a woman who has stuck by my side through thick and thin. I shared my brain gremlin thoughts with her... because sharing these thoughts with someone who can truly hold space for me (and for whom I return the favor) *takes their power away.*

"Either you can accept the discomfort of growth or you can fight it. Either way, it's going to happen. It's up to you how easy or hard it will be," she said.

My response, via text, was something along the lines of:

She shot back with, "Mental to do list. GO."

"Brush teeth. Wash face. Apply makeup. Temper tantrum. Pray. Get dressed. Put Floyd in crate. Go." I responded.

I went to the meeting. Upon sitting down with the gentleman, I felt a wave of peace. Within five minutes of talking, I realized that we were, like, the same breed of human. We had been through similar awakenings. We had both survived the withdrawal of antidepressants. We spoke the same language. We *got* each other on a soul level.

Publisher told me he'd been reading my 30 Days of Seeking God blog and that he was *enjoying* it and *relating to it* and that I was a good writer. *He said that last part twice, with intense eye contact to make sure that I was listening.* He commended my honesty and vulnerability. "You're doing it," he said. And I totally knew what he meant by "it." **I am doing what I've always dreamed of doing. I am helping people (including myself) through my writing.**

Typing that sends tingles down my arms and into my fingertips. I want to do spirit fingers or jazz hands in celebration.

spirit fingers

And then he asked me to be a part of his magazine's writing team.

jazz hands

And *then* we started talking about the book I wanted to write. His response?

"I want to publish your book."

"What? Really?" I asked.

"Write the book. I will publish it."

In the very moment of writing the account of this interaction, I had this silent moment of awe. Publication is something that used to stress me out to the point of *not* writing because I assumed I'd never get published. The people who used to say, "Do what you love and the rest will fall into place" pissed me off. However, during my journey of authentic sharing and doing what I love, doors are truly opening where there seemed to be walls before.

Here's what being on the writing team and getting my book published mean to me: I get to share my heart with more people. I get to help people through their awakenings. I get to spread the message of love, of awareness, and of oneness. It isn't about how many likes I get, or even about how many copies I sell. It is about sharing my messy, authentic truth with the intention of helping others embrace *their* messy truths.

Of course, Inner Saboteur was all like, "OH BIG WOOP. I'M SURE ALL WRITERS ARE PARTS OF LOCAL MAGAZINE

WRITING TEAMS." And "It's a small, local publishing company. A MAX OF 20 PEOPLE WILL READ YOUR BOOK."

I quickly hushed the voice. I instead congratulated myself aloud on this exciting step in my journey. I shared with the people closest to me *who I knew would embrace me with excitement.* My old habit was to immediately reach out to fun sponges whenever something exciting happened.

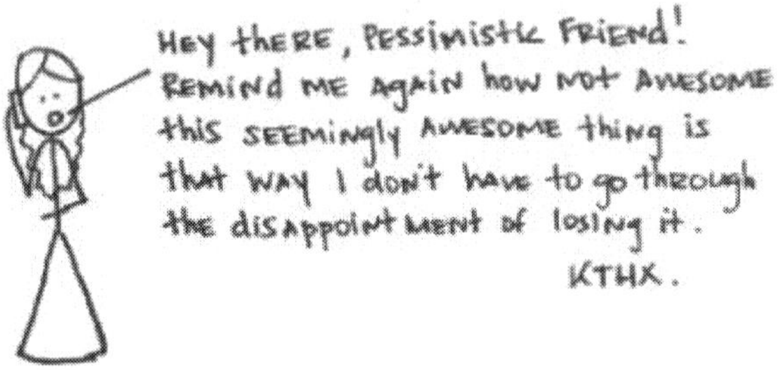
Hey there, Pessimistic Friend!
Remind me again how not awesome this seemingly awesome thing is that way I don't have to go through the disappointment of losing it.
KTHX.

This time, I shared with folks who I knew would be supportive. Then I thanked this God character... A lot.

And this is how I know some sort of higher realm of existence (that I choose to call God) exists today. Because I sort of figured my career as a writer would be posting occasionally popular FB posts and getting a few more articles published to online magazines and that'd be the extent of it. Sure, I still held out hope for the dream of having my books published, but that seemed *so far away.*

All of the sudden, that dream is less blurry. I had this explosion of realization that was like "OH WHOA. I've had that dream since I was a kid for a reason. It's because it's what I'm freakin' *here to do."*

AND I'M DOING IT. I am sharing openly and vulnerably and with as much awareness as I have at any given moment. Even though I oftentimes look back at posts from three months prior and am like "I had no idea what I was talking about" or "I sound like a know-it-all bitch," I STILL AM WRITING. I STILL AM SHARING.

Because we are all works in progress. We need more reminders of that in life, yknow? Let's let go

Ancora Imparo

of this ideal of perfection and instead embrace where we are *right now.* Because where we are right now **IS ENOUGH.**

~ * ~

The 30 Days of Seeking God also got me into the rooms of Alcoholics Anonymous. A large part of the success of AA is based upon being based on attraction rather than promotion. As such, I won't go into heavy detail about the program. I will say that I aptly avoided it for many years. Looking back, I now remember at least two therapists recommending AA to me. I refused to go. *That was for people with a drinking problem. I didn't have a drinking problem. I had a living problem.*

Once I decided to embark upon the God journey, I prayed and meditated for some form of guidance. I wanted guidelines or a to do list. What came through was shocking: Go to a 12-step meeting every day for thirty days. This seemingly came out of nowhere. I had occasionally visited a local NA (Narcotics Anonymous) meeting, but I certainly didn't see the need for me going every single day. After all, I hadn't had alcohol or pills in nearly two years. I clearly knew what I was doing.

Even so, I listened. I went to a meeting of young folks around my age. I sat in the corner of the room, in as small of a ball as I could. I was closed off. I was terrified. I was certain that none of these people could *possibly* understand me. Some talked of DUIs. Others talked of prison. Nearly everyone cussed. I felt uncomfortable, like the new girl in school. I spent much of the meeting judging those in the room, since most of them were consuming energy drinks, frou-frou Boodles drinks which were *clearly* packed with cream and sugar, and smoking from vape e-cigarette things. *These people don't know,* I thought. *They have no idea about the importance of food and how that can retrain the brain not to drink.*

I was certain that I had it all figured out. I could control *my* addiction.

I guess this God character had a different plan for me.

After the meeting ended, a few young women surrounded me. This confused me greatly. *Do they not feel the energetic spikes I'm sending at them? NOT INTERESTED, LADIES. Move along.* They weren't fazed. They introduced themselves to me, they hugged me, and a girl offered to be my temporary sponsor. She said she'd give me a to do list of what I needed to do every day. I got my notebook out in preparation to write the list.

"Call me tomorrow," she said, with a smile.

"That way I can see that you're dedicated."

Challenge: accepted.

I called her the next day and was given my list. Every day, I needed to:

-Call my sponsor and be honest about my feelings.

-Call three women in recovery and ask how *their* days were going.

-Pray morning and night.

-Read a specific excerpt from the recommended AA text (known as "The Big Book") morning and night.

-Go to a meeting. She recommended at least 3-5 times a week. (The regular recommendation I've heard has been 90 meetings in 90 days. I decided to stick with my 30 in 30 days and re-evaluate thereafter.)

I was mostly terrified about the idea of calling three women a day. Clearly Sponsor didn't understand that I'd once had a nervous breakdown when working a job where I called strangers every day. I had been doing all of my intuitive work via email and Facebook in order to avoid phone calls. The *last* thing I wanted was to talk to strangers—especially women—on the phone.

But, I did it, because, naturally, I wanted to be the best sponsee ever.

There are twelve steps in AA and a similar form in each 12-step program. I recommend asking Google about them. One of the primary elements required for recovery is rigorous honesty. Honesty alone is scary, but *rigorous* honesty? Now that's a whole deeper level. I truly believe that every single human being would benefit from going through a 12-step program. There are support groups for alcoholics, addicts, folks with eating disorders, people who've been abused, and the list goes on. My description of 12-step programs is this: They're a safe place to go and to, step by step, be introduced to who you truly are underneath all of the baggage and masks and scars and fibs.

Also, it's a way to experience God.

And I do not mean a religious God. I had one person reach out to me after I began my journey of seeking God to say, "Jen, I'm so glad you've decided to seek out the Christian God." I was like, *Uuuuhhhh. What? I don't want any limiting title next to God. K? No Zeus beard and lightning bolt, either. Get that shit outta' here.*

To me, that's like me telling folks that I'm on a 30-day journey of seeking cake and having someone say, "I'm so glad you've decided to seek out strawberry cake!" No, Lady. No. I don't want to be limited to strawberry cake. Sure, I bet it's delicious. However, I want to try *all* of the cake. Then, I can decide on my own personal favorite that is most delicious to me.

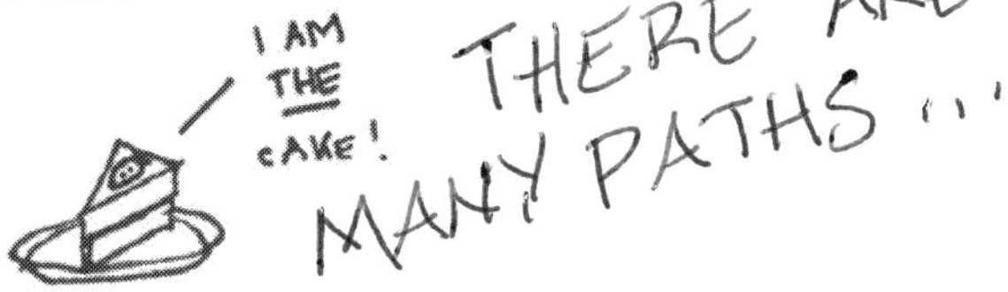

My journey was to arrive at my own personal understanding of this higher power. Some days, I prayed to the painting in my bedroom. It was one I'd done left-handed as part of an artist's date with Little Jen. *At least I know* ***you*** *exist,* I used to think toward the painting.

Sponsor and I met once per week at Boodles. She drank a green drink and I ordered a hot water and brought my own tea. We took turns reading from The Big Book, switching off after each page. I was embarrassed at first. *We're in public,* I thought. *People can hear us.* I remember seeing a relatively attractive man and thinking, *Well. There go my chances with him. Now he'll know I'm an alcoholic.*

I really struggled to call myself an alcoholic or an addict in meetings. That's part of the approach. "My name is NAME and I'm an alcoholic/addict." To which everyone else responds in unison: "Hiiii, NAAAAME." If words are prayers, then I didn't want to further perpetuate this addict mentality by regularly calling myself one. I avoided speaking for my first week or so in meetings.

Then, something happened. I started to relax into my body. Hearing other people share about their experience, strength, hope, and occasional bat-shittery helped me feel hopeful. It helped me feel less alone. I became less tense. I isolated less. By calling three women each day, I began making friends. And these were not friends that I was making via some façade. These women liked me for me.

Praying was working. I logically tried to figure out *why* it was working. *Maybe it's because I'm divorcing myself from incessant worry by giving my concerns to this mystical God, thereby allowing my vibration to come into alignment with my true divine path.* Or *maybe it's because I'm becoming clear on my wants and needs, so the Universe has something to work off of.*

I soon realized that, although I had begun my thirty-day journey looking for an intellectual understanding and an idea of God, what I got was much more powerful. I have been gifted with an experience of God.

Sharing my feelings in a room of twenty or more people has given me practice with inspirational speaking, which is something I dream of doing. I don't intend for my public speaking to be preachy. I want it to be real. Sharing in a room full of alcoholics and addicts and fellow crazies, I have found myself feeling more and more comfortable sharing from a place of honesty and vulnerability. About a month ago, I realized that **I am ready** to do public speaking. For a long time, I was hung up on the idea of not being healed enough or confident enough or thin enough to have people listen to me.

My experience has been that, the more vulnerable and authentic I am in my sharing (and the less I try to plan out what I'm going to say before saying it), the more my words resonate with people.

As I write this, I am working on step eight, which is to make a list of all people I have harmed. Step nine is to make amends to these people. I am thrilled to begin this process and yet, simultaneously, I want to spoon Floyd underneath my comforter and sleep until it's all over with.

Here is my [still-limited] understanding of what the last two months of AA has done for me: Before entering AA, I was sober, but I was not *recovering.* I focused on the physical portion of my addictions. I ate the right and best foods, got enough sleep, exercised semi-regularly, meditated, journaled, did positive affirmations, and many other actions which certainly have assisted my healing. However, any time I skipped one or more of these daily to-do list items, I dealt with anxiety. I feared I'd suddenly go crazy and try to kill myself. I was managing my symptoms rather than getting to the root cause and healing there.

One of my favorite sayings that I've heard is "We are only as sick as our secrets." With how hard I've been on myself (and others) throughout my life and with how deeply I suppressed my emotions, it was no wonder that I had dealt with so much sickness. The physical pain, the emotional turmoil, the suicidality, etc. All of these, I've found, are *messages*. They are invitations to look deeper at what truly needs to be addressed.

Alcoholics Anonymous gave me a safe place to stretch out my wings. It gave me a safe ground to express myself in whatever place I happened to be in any given moment. There were nights that I'd go into a meeting certain I was the only person feeling the way I felt. Through hearing other people share their stories, though, I realized I wasn't alone.

~ * ~

Something I have hinted toward but have yet to dive into has been the topic of my channeling. I believe this hesitation and avoidance has been fear-based. First, it's a fear because I logically do not fully understand how it works. My Skeptic maintains a constant Resting Bitch Face at the thought of setting my consciousness aside and allowing a group of high-vibrational non-physical beings to talk through me.

In my very first session with Mentor, as I mentioned earlier, she told me that I was a channel. She told me to start practicing channeling by recording my voice on my phone.

"Don't think about what you're saying," she explained, "Just talk and let it flow."

Much like this book.

I began doing so. I had been unknowingly channeling via my writing ever since my March 2014 chat with Archangel Michael. Heck, it likely occurred prior to that point without me knowing to call it that. In my journaling and morning pages, I posed questions to my Higher Self and angels and whomever else was listening. Then, without thinking, I'd begin writing an answer without stopping. Interestingly enough, the responses would refer to me as "Dear One" and used the pronoun of "you" rather than "I." The advice that came through was always spot on with what I needed to hear… And it was always way above my conscious level of awareness.

Now. Even with the last nearly two years of journeying through this awakening, my Skeptic program still runs. Sometimes, Skeptic tells me that these spirit guides don't exist and that it's all *me* making up the channeled work.

Maybe that *is* the case. Although, if so? That'd mean I am all kinds of wise and smart and patient and loving, all of the time. In fact, it'd be more of a compliment to me and my ego if these beings *didn't* exist.

I remember when I sat my mom down to break the news to her that I was a channel. It was hard for me to accept and embrace any sort of intuitive abilities. Since I initially struggled to believe in them, I hesitated to speak to anyone about my spiritual experiences. In this instance with my mom, thought, I didn't hold back or mold at all. I explained that I have a connection and receive messages from high vibrational non-physical beings (such as angels or spirit guides) and that it's my divine path to share these messages with people to help raise the energetic vibration of the earth. I told her that I didn't believe it at first, but that enough situations have happened for me to be a believer.

I chose to speak with my mom because she's pretty open-minded and connected to her intuition. My dad is where I got my left-brained dominance from, so I figured it'd be an easier route to chat with Mom. Even so, I still expected some type of kickback. Instead, she listened intently and nodded, as if I was telling her about the casserole I made the other night.

Out of nowhere, my dad walks into the room and goes, "Mama B was a channel." (Mama B was his grandma.)

"REALLY?!" I asked.

My mom nodded and goes, "I've known you had this gift since you were born. Especially since you were a kid. I knew you were meant to share your gift and help people."

I sat there with this sideways dog face of confusion because I totally expected them to call me crazy. Instead they sat there, one sipping beer and the other munching cheesecake, talking to me about my channeling abilities and the best way for me to make a living with them.

"Why has no one told me this in the past?!" I finally asked.

"Jen," my mom responded, "You were an atheist. You didn't believe in any of this."

"Oh. Yes. That's right."

This has taught me a rather valuable lesson. Throughout most of my life, I held back many facets of myself and instead shared what I figured would be accepted. Meanwhile, I was hermiting at home with my unspoken truths, feeling isolated and alone. Each

WHY WOULD BEING AN ATHEIST MEAN ONE WOULD NOT BELIEVE IN "ANY OF THIS." ???

time I push myself out of my comfort zone and share some previously unspoken truths, I am pleasantly surprised by the outcome. Has my honesty pushed people away? Absolutely. I'd like to think that this process makes space for the people who can and will appreciate my approach to writing and sharing.

By now, you've gotten a feel for my writing style. Here's an example of channeled writing from a group of spirit guides I work with that I call The Rebels. This is a part of "Activation Code," a fully channeled book I started in February 2015.

There is hope. There is always hope. There is no need to dwell on shortcomings as many do, as this only brings more attention to those aspects of self that are less than preferable. You've likely heard that what you put your attention on grows. Not only does it grow, but it also becomes stronger. Its vibration becomes more attractive. Like-minded humans and situations will be attracted to whichever emotion most strongly vibrates. If you find yourself fending off bouts of anger and temper tantrums, you will be attracting more people, situations, and behaviors that reinforce your feelings of anger.

If, on the other hand, you surround yourself with that which fills you with joy and happiness, you will open the window of possibility to allow the cool, refreshing breeze of positivity to caress your skin.

A topic that seems to cause much dismay is the belief that taking the time to embark upon journeys of joy, laughter, and fun is actually a waste of time. A distraction. We assure you that this is far from the case.

People think, if I am drawing with sidewalk chalk and playing hopscotch, how on earth is that helping me reach my professional goals? *We are grateful that you asked. When you make the time to blow bubbles or play in puddles or doodle or dance to a favorite song, you are adjusting your vibration closer to its natural state. This state is one of peace, enjoyment, and open receptivity.*

Your natural way of existence is to be in the flow. Your struggles and your furrowed brow and your copious amounts of stress-filled sighs are all products of your environment and have absolutely nothing to do with who you truly are. Your dreams and aspirations stem from your true self. As such, you must rediscover this part of you. Once you have, your life will be in a constant state of flow.

I started sharing short channeled videos via a YouTube channel and sharing excerpts from Activation Code on Facebook or in my blog. However, as I have frequently done in the past, I would post regularly for a week or two and then hibernate in the safety of my bed, underneath my down comforter, fully avoiding anything to do with sharing with the outside world. And, now that I've openly called myself on my shit, I've little choice but to make and post more videos.

I suppose that every type of creative expression is channeled, when it comes down to it. Even if something isn't channeled from a higher realm, it can be channeled from a certain part of ourselves. For instance, my inner truth is being channeled into this writing. My dream of having a book published before the age of 30 is being channeled through the words. You reading these words allows you to absorb the forward momentum of this energy.

~ * ~

For so long, I judged the success or validity of my words based off of the response to them. If I got 20+ "likes" on a post, I felt accepted and safe and motivated to share more. If I got 1 (or even 0, which has happened), I'd feel deflated and immediately assume that countless people had seen the post and hated it and were holding a secret meeting to discuss how insane I was and that everything I said was crap.

I smile as I write this, because I've recently become aware of a wonderful truth: I am not the most important person in the world. I am neither above nor beneath anyone. Other folks have *way* too much going on to stress themselves out over what I'm doing and posting about on social media. There have been plenty of times when I've scrolled through and read something odd on another's wall. You know what I did about it? I kept scrolling and very quickly lost interest in the oddness I'd just read. Or, if it was extra quirky, I may have clicked further and done approximately three minutes of Facebook or Instagram stalking in an effort to appease my inherently nosy nature. I wouldn't send a mass email out to people to point out how weird I thought this person was. In fact, within minutes, my busy brain would have found something else to obsess over.

This applies to others as well. That is to say that, even when someone disagrees with what I'm saying and thinks I am kooky, *it doesn't matter.* That person will not obsess over it. And heck, if they do? Then that's totally reflective of something on *their* end and, frankly, is none of my business.

I remember the first time I had a few people un-like my professional Facebook page. I was *heartbroken.* My oh my, was I hurt. Also, even though

I had been irregularly posting to YouTube and had yet (and have yet) to find a solid direction for my videos, I managed to get over 30 subscribers. This motivated me, until someone *un-subscribed*. When that happened, I immediately avoided posting another video for over a month.

A MONTH. BECAUSE OF ONE PERSON.

And who knows why they un-subscribed? Maybe it was an accident. Maybe they didn't know they were already subscribed and, upon hitting the button to subscribe to the channel, they unknowingly un-subscribed themselves. Maybe I reminded them of their 2nd grade teacher who went overkill on the time-outs. Maybe they disagreed with a post. Maybe they found me boring.

And guess what.

I do not care.

I truly mean this. I now see things in a vibrational sense. We're all energy, right? With that in mind, as I become more in vibrational alignment with my divine path, it makes sense for certain people to fall away. We are no longer on the same wavelength. This is neither good nor bad; it merely means that our paths are no longer beneficial to one another. During the weeding out process, more room is being created for those who are in alignment with my goals and dreams… And I for them.

This is something that Mentor helped me realize. She explained that, when she let go of a part of her business (which was energetically draining for her and brought little income but many followers loved), a large chunk of people opted out of her mailing list. Through some effort, she was able to view this positively. I have thankfully adopted this mindset.

You know what it took to get me to this level of comfort and understanding? Rejection. Hurt feelings. Discomfort.

Realistically, all of those ouchy experiences were a part of the writing of this book. I needed a certain level of okayness with the possibility (and inevitability) of someone rejecting or disliking or ignoring what I share before feeling confident enough to finish a book. I am sure there are more layers of healing regarding this. The only way to arrive at those layers of healing is to continue pushing through the discomfort, allow myself to recalibrate to my growth, and then continue onward again.

At the time of me writing this portion of the book, I have no idea what my channeling is going to look like. I'd like to think that this book has been channeled, in a sense. It's been channeled from my true self, from my core, rather than edited by the hands of my ego, Skeptic, or Censor. Maybe this is the type of channeling I will do. Rather than stress myself out over it, though, I've decided to continue doing what I know to do: write. As I create and listen, I am led. One day, my YouTube channel will make sense. Or maybe it won't. Either way, worrying about it will accomplish nothing.

And so, I write.

~ * ~

I remember right before my 29th birthday, I hardcore poured myself into finishing my memoir. I wanted to do so *before* my birthday. When I put deadlines on things, it's as though a fire is lit beneath my ass. It helps motivate me to get stuff done, especially if the deadline is, like, tomorrow. At 8AM.

I started sharing small excerpts once per week on Facebook and the response was *amazing.* Creative non-fiction writing had always been my specialty.

Once I began the transition into this spiritual chapter of my life, I first went *really* extreme with it. I stopped cussing for a while. I limited myself to posting spiritual writing that could've only been appropriately read in the breathy voice of a soft-spoken yoga instructor. There was total truth behind what I was saying, but it was *not* authentic. This has been an interesting balance to discover. So, upon sharing excerpts of my story, people reacted positively. I had re-introduced my humor and my sarcasm, neither of which I initially thought were "allowed" in a spiritual way of life.

Everyone responded well, except for a few people who were close to me. Why? Because what I posted *was about them.* The stories were about memories from my childhood and were told in a very straight-forward way and from *my* point of view. Also, they were the epitome of unedited. I remember sending excerpts to my family with the attached motivation of "SEE? I *have* been writing and working hard this entire time! Look at what I've accomplished! GIVE ME APPROVAL!"

As such, that is the opposite of what I got.

The responses consisted of hurt feelings and a few folks telling me to share *less.* (One or more people have told me to write fiction instead of non-fiction. They claim that an audience would be more likely to accept my writing if it was labeled as fictitious.) Those who had been involved in the memories exclaimed, "It didn't happen that way!"

That's the funny thing about truth. Ten people can experience the *exact* same situation and all come out with a different interpretation. As such, all would be telling the truth from their memory, even if each story discounted the other.

As per usual, their responses were promptly organized into the "NEGATIVE" pile and I completely avoided my memoir… For months. I spoke with my dad about it, who was one of the few people who responded with deep love and support. I have his words of wisdom (which arrived via text) written on a sticky note which lives on my office wall, directly beneath the light switch and to the left of my Censor. It reads:

> *Write or die.*
> *Do not seek approval from your family and friends.*
> *You will never get it.*
> *Or you will get it but not believe it.*
> *Or you will receive bad reviews and it will deflate your energies.*
> *You much create for yourself and let others discover it.*

Preach, Pops. Preach.

Perhaps the first sentence seems a little extreme. *WRITE OR DIE!* But to me, it's true. Writing is more than a hobby; it's my freaking life force. I believe that expression is essential for all humans, but I can only speak for myself. I *know* that expression is essential for my survival. When I don't write, my life becomes stagnant, stale, boring, and barren. When I do write, my life remains plush and lush and vibrant. More than anything, it remains *honest.* Rigorous honesty, although difficult to initially adopt, is one of the most beautiful parts of my life now. Life is *way less stressful* now that I tell the truth all of the time.

Also, in relation to having taken a few months away from the memoir due to ouchy feelings and fear of hurting others with my words, *this time away also attributed to the writing of this book.* For it was during this time that I lowered and subsequently ceased medication. This helped me get even more in touch with my deeper, darker emotions. It helped me finally begin shedding self-pity. As such, the same stories I was telling five months ago can now be told in a different light. They are still the same stories, but my level of awareness allows me to interpret them in a more loving and balanced way.

Rather than interpreting an event as something having happened to me (as a victim), I now see events as opportunities to experience and learn from. This shift allows each and every day to be enjoyable in its own way. Even if I'm in a cranky mindset, I still find myself grumbling, "There'd better be a lesson involved here." And there is. There always is.

There is a trust that I experience now, which is still rather new for me. Even when I'm feeling uncomfortable or as though life is a chaotic mess, I now choose to trust that something is being worked out inside of me that I simply do not yet have the conscious awareness to comprehend. So, rather than stress about it or try to force *my* will by attempting to manage every little aspect of my life, I pray to whatever/whomever is listening (which I often call God), and I let go. I choose to instead stay in the moment.

To be clear, this is still a daily challenge for me. Earlier today, for instance, I spent two hours attempting to convince myself to get out of bed. I pounded my fists and kicked my feet while having a temper tantrum. Yea. A nearly-30-year-old.

Having a temper tantrum. Flailing and squealing and pouting. It happened.

Finally, I surrendered. And it sounded something like this: "FINE, God. FINE. Clearly my ideas about what I should be doing simply aren't working. So. If you want me to lie here in bed in the middle of the afternoon and do nothing *even though I have a bunch I should be doing*, then fine. I'll do it. I'll trust that there is some unseen reason for this stillness. And I'll stay put until you give me some intuitive thought or action to do otherwise. Okay? Okay." I believe this was followed by a dramatic sigh and eye roll.

Within five minutes, I had the inspiration to get out of bed, get dressed, and take Floyd for a walk.

~ * ~

I have been struggling through a bout of depression over the last few days of writing this. And you know what? I'm actually excited to be *in* this depressive state while working on this book so that I can explain this state of mind and heart while in the midst of the experience.

I feel damp. You know when you wash towels and overload them into the dryer so that they need more than one cycle to dry? I feel like a towel in between dry cycle one and two. It's still a towel. It still could absorb more moisture. But it certainly isn't the ideal state for a towel. And, if left for too long, it gets cold. And smelly.

I'm still Jen. I'm just a cold, damp version of Jen right now.

When I get into these states, I have many thought gerbils running through my head. First, there is the thought of *Oh no, what if there actually is something "wrong" with me?* And, *What if I'm going to be like this forever? What if, without medication, this is what I'm like?*

This is proof that old habits and beliefs are stubborn. What I have learned (and am still very much in the process of integrating) is that my feeling uncomfortable and damp is not indicative of something being *wrong* with me. Just because I'm experiencing discomfort does not equate to this being a bad experience. As with any journey, life has its ups and downs and lefts and rights. The important part is to take one step after another, even when feeling like a smelly damp washcloth.

It is through discomfort that one is able to grow. If that's the case—which I truly believe it to be—then I'm growing a *lot* right now. I feel uncomfortable and frustrated and antsy. The mean brain gerbil that is the loudest is saying the following: *How can you possibly help other depressed people when you're still depressed yourself?*

And to you, Bully Gerbil, I say this: *I know that, when I'm in dark places, it is helpful to be shown that other people experience similar emotions. This helps me feel less alone. It is my hope and belief that this book will help others in a similar way. Realistically, I believe I am most helpful to other depressed people because I understand how they feel. Also, my approach is to utilize the energy in a creative fashion rather than to numb it or hide it, and I believe this stands to be a very beneficial approach for others.*

Look at Glennon Doyle Melton, for example. She is a self-proclaimed clinically depressed motivational speaker. She uses the energy of her anxiety to share vulnerably and in a way that touches other people's hearts. This is healing and helpful to all who read her blog or attend her speaking engagements. My job is to share openly, honestly, and vulnerably, regardless of my state of mind. That is what I vow to do.

I find it rather helpful to stand up to the gerbils and put them in their place. Realistically, I'm standing up for myself *to* myself.

HOW I FEEL AFTER
STANDING UP TO GERBIL:

Standing up for myself to myself was rather difficult when I first started doing it a little over a year ago. Before that, I was a hardcore bully. I made fun of myself, I called myself mean names, and I berated myself about how fat or lazy or ugly or lame or unloved I was. In fact, the only way I would stand up for myself at first was to imagine that I was standing up for Lil' Jen, a much younger version of me. It was (and is) much easier to protect and console this adorable, quirky little girl than my present-day self:

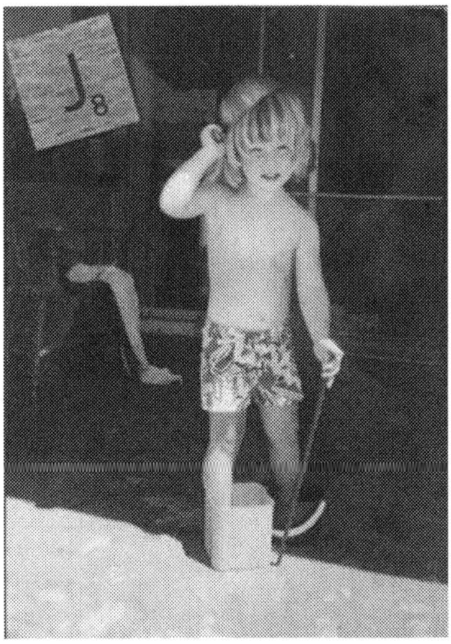

My belief is that, as kids, we are open and vulnerable and sensitive. And, when some kind of trauma or pain occurs, we create some sort of limiting belief as a result. This is in an effort to protect ourselves from that type of pain occurring again. This becomes part of our programming and, by the time we're a couple decades older, we may assume this limited thinking is *just who we are.* I beg to differ.

I think that, when triggered in a similar fashion to earlier pain, a person may emotionally/mentally regress to the emotional maturity of that younger age. When two people in a relationship are fighting, for example, it seems common for both to be fighting as a younger, less mature version of themselves.

I am nearing thirty years old as a single woman and therefore am not in a place to offer relationship advice, but I will say that standing up for and taking care of that inner child aspect of myself has been an integral part of my healing process. I can only imagine that, if both members of a couple took the time to do this, it'd be beneficial to the relationship.

I was so detached from myself when I first began this self-love journey two years ago that it felt impossible to love (or even like) myself. It was easy, however, to love that sweet and smiley little kid version of me. Sometimes I still get to that place of feeling snarky toward my current self. When that occurs, the process looks a little like this:

Oftentimes, when someone (including me) says something that feels hurtful, I have no idea how to begin to stand up for myself. I get into a self-pity mode and agree with the comment. This happens immediately. It feels as though there's very little time to shift the process toward a positive or loving experience. As soon as the negative thought happens, I feel myself having agreed with it and having accepted it as truth. If I imagine a cute little blonde girl with buckets on her feet and a dog bowl on her head, though, the pause button is easy to push. From there, I'm able to reword the empowered statement in order to apply it to my present-day self.

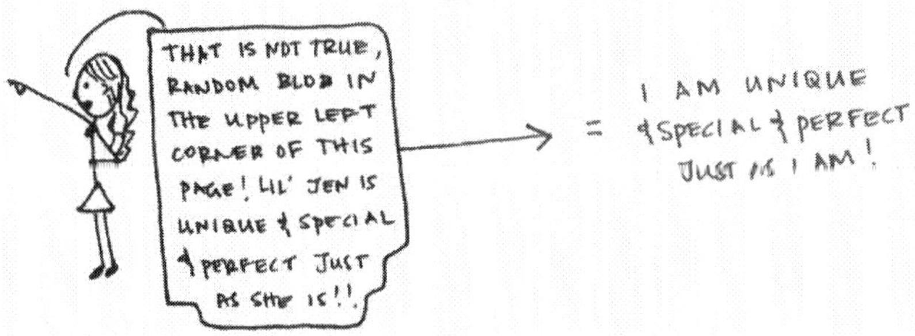

After doodling all of that and inserting it into this document, I let out a big sigh of relief. I am unique and special and perfect just as I am. You are unique and special and perfect just as you are. And if that's tough to believe, then imagine saying it to a much younger version of yourself, before you learned to dislike yourself.

~ * ~

What I really want to say is that I'm scared. I've been hiding. I was riding the flow of this book and then went into editing mode once it felt mostly completed. That resulted in confusion for me because there is so much involved in this book. I have spent the last few days attempting to define it. *Do I remove the daily journal entries describing how my life has transpired during the writing of this book? Do I have it be a self-help book and put the memoir into a separate document?*

And the answer just came to me: quite simply, no. I should not remove anything.

CENSOR: *But isn't that you being lazy? Publishers won't want to deal with such a messy book.*

ME: It's not me being lazy. It is me trusting that what has come through me during the last four weeks is exactly what some folks need to read. It's allowing my authentic voice to be expressed as is, without being boxed in.

I've been irritable and discontent lately. I even arrived at a pretty heavy bout of suicidality the other night. This felt frustrating to me. My old program told me that this was a failure.

CENSOR: *How can you write a book to help others survive their suicidality and darkness when you're still dealing with yours?*

JEN: I can help others through their darkness and suicidality by sharing openly about mine. I will not hide from it. I will not remain in a state of shame about it.

And honestly? That's where I've been. While going through and doing the first light edit of this book, I found myself drawing my comfortable control walls around the book and around myself. I started to feel claustrophobic. I started to want to be preachy and teach-y with my writing rather than being raw and messy.

But, in my opinion, there is enough surface-level preachy stuff out there. That's not what this book is for. This entire book has been me utilizing emotional energy *in order to create.* I've compiled over 65,000 words within four weeks by utilizing the energy of my darkness (and at times my light), so I'd venture to say that my bathtub's advice was correct. Onward, Passion Wagon!

~ * ~

When I first quit drinking, I was introduced to waves of emotion and memories that I'd never before felt because I'd been numbing them for so long. And now, three months after weaning off of anti-depressants, I've been introduced to yet another set of emotions and memories that I've never before felt.

The trick is to realize that I'm not stuck here. This is deeply difficult at times because of how freaking *sour* and painful depression is. Truly, when in the midst of a depressive episode, I become *absolutely certain* that nothing else exists. *This is how life actually is,* I think, *and all of the serenity I was experiencing prior to this was false.*

Something Therapist II (an amazing woman I started seeing after the breakup with Actor) taught me the importance of defining what it is that I'm feeling. I was so out of touch with my emotions for so long that I didn't know what they were. I viewed them in a binary way. They were either good or bad. They were either enjoyable or painful. She actually gave me a printout of a Feeling Wheel which lists lots of different emotions on it. From there, I was to pick one emotion that I was feeling every day and express it aloud.

This was difficult at first. Sometimes, it still is.

See, I spent my whole life relying on my intellect, ignoring the language of my emotions. At times, when I'm sitting with all of these sensations that I don't recognize, I feel like I've been placed right smack in the middle of an Advanced French class while I know roughly eleven words in French.

In fact, this is sort of how I feel about most of my life. I don't feel like I fit in. I feel as though everyone else is fluent in Human and I am in desperate need of a tutor. (Maybe that's what my therapist is—a tutor for Humaning.) Last night, I did something really difficult and different. After the 10PM AA meeting I normally go to, I didn't speed walk out to my car as soon as the meeting closed. *I stayed.*

And boy, did I feel awkward.

Most people left, but a handful stayed behind and huddled in the middle of the room on the array of mis-matched couches. I remained with that handful. My mind raced and I felt ridiculous and like I should be talking or laughing or doing *some*thing. I didn't know what to do with my hands. I think I sat on them… Or used them to cover the belly roll that has recently begun joining me when I sit down.

I had a mini quantum leap of realization. It's one I've had before, but I integrate it more deeply each time this happens.

What if everyone feels just as awkward as I do? And if not now, what if they did at one time? What if I'm not wrong or weird for feeling the way I do? What if these uncomfortable emotions are *normal?*

Well that'd be wild, wouldn't it?

So, in the spirit of rigorous honesty, I utilized the energy of my social anxiety to tell everyone how awkward I felt. I tried this at a friend's daughter's birthday party a couple weeks ago and it wasn't received very well. The people I told at the party were what I refer to as Civilians. Sometimes I call them Earthlings. These are the people who either have yet to begin awakening or are adept at hiding it. As such, when I said, "Whew! My social anxiety is through the roof. I am sweating profusely. What about you?" The responses were mostly furrowed brows and awkward shuffles.

But! Last night, when I shared among other rigorously honest people about how awkward I felt, they all explained that they, too, had dealt with such social anxiety. One guy told me he would shake when around people, all the way into his second year of sobriety. Another girl (who didn't stay after with us) wrote me a text that said, "I feel so f*cking stupid. I get so awkward. I don't know what to say, so I just walk away."

This solidified it for me: EVERYONE DEALS WITH AWKWARDNESS AND UNCOMFORTABLE EMOTIONS.

I've simply a tendency to compare my uncomfortable insides to what people are portraying on the outside. *What if all of these other folks are so busy managing their own discomfort that they don't even recognize mine?*

Oh my, that sure is a freeing thought.

Something else Therapist II has taught me is that emotions are like the weather. They come and go. They fluctuate. When a really bad storm comes, my reaction isn't a meltdown of "Oh no! This storm is going to last forever! It has always been like this and it always will be like this! I should give up. I'll never see the sunshine again."

Sometimes I can anticipate rainstorms. Other times I can't. Sometimes I think a conversation or situation will trigger me into an emotional meltdown but I end up handling it rather well. This is like when the forecast says it's going to rain all weekend but it's suddenly sunny instead. The opposite also holds true. What I've learned about weather in Georgia is to completely release attachment to expectations. Perhaps the same holds true to myself and my feelings.

I have emotions, but I am not my emotions. If I have an entire day of socializing planned and I wake up to a surprise storm cloud of depression, this doesn't mean that my day is ruined. It may be different than anticipated, but it can still be a good day. *I can still have an okay day, even if I'm feeling depressed.*

~ * ~

I'd like to think that, once I get accustomed to this new wave of emotion that has come to me since quitting anti-depressants and my brain chemicals get nice and balanced, I will be in a more regular state of contentment. I imagine that my journey of self-discovery and recovery is much like cleaning a hoarder's house. One seemingly small closet in my mind holds a *lot* of old, stagnant stuff. Cleaning and organizing such a place will take time and patience and even a sense of humor. There is a lot that is being processed and worked out inside of me that my conscious mind may not understand. All my conscious mind sees is *I am less happy than I was a few months ago. Maybe that means I need medication.*

My response to that is: I have been on medication since I was thirteen years old. I've been off of it for a mere three months. I'm essentially rebuilding atrophied muscles. It will take time to learn how to handle life in its fullness. There will be days when I'm too sore to exercise, or perhaps too depressed to get out of bed. The key, for me, is to remove the judgment.

Today, for instance, I found myself taking a depressive nap in the afternoon in order to escape how uncomfortable life has felt for me lately. This is something I'd have previously been upset at myself about. Instead, I accepted it. Rather than fight myself on the nap and invite self-pity to join me (thereby extending the nap from 30 minutes to an all-day affair), I accepted it. *Fine,* I thought. *This is where I am now. This is what I need now. I may not like it or understand it, but I am choosing to accept it.*

Is it ideal? Being a nearly 30-year-old single woman experiencing the ups and downs of depression who oftentimes feels like she can't get out of bed in the morning? No. But it's where I am, and I accept that.

What's more is that *I take action.* There may be times when taking physical action seems impossible. In those cases, I work to switch my thought pattern from lack to gratitude, or I pray, or I say affirmations that I barely believe. I write. Maybe all I can do is floss. That's okay too. Today I took a shower, washed my hair, and put on nice clothes. *That is a win for me.*

I have found that it's important to celebrate small victories. It is each consistent step that takes us closer to our freedom. And, just like when learning a new language, it's imperative that I allow myself this time to build the foundation. I must allow myself room to stumble as I figure out the basics of this new, louder volume of life. Rather than get caught up in how I wish I was or how I hope I'll eventually be, I repeatedly remind myself to accept where I am *right now.*

I once read that my fighting the present moment (however uncomfortable) is my fighting the Universe. And, although I do consider myself stocky and strong, I'm somewhat certain that the Universe is more powerful than I am.

The visual that just popped into my head was that of a map. Perhaps life is simply one big road trip. There are times of exciting adventures and other times of barren, boring road for many miles. There are surprise storms and flat tires. There are beautiful states and there are rough parts of town that need maintenance. Maybe life has been set up as this multi-faceted, long term road trip. Maybe it's not at all about some final destination but rather about enjoying every little stop.

~ * ~

We have survived 100% of our worst days thus far. Truly, we have a 100% survival rate. This is important for me to keep in mind, especially when I'm experiencing the intense sourness of depression.

There are many reasons depression pops up, I've found. Sometimes it's to do with the season. Other times it's because I've been slacking on my daily self-care or not eating enough vegetables (which help sustain balanced energy and mood). Occasionally it's because I haven't reinforced energetic boundaries and have some needy spirits sucking my energy dry. Other times, still, it's because the girl at Starbucks is prettier than me, married, and somehow has zero cellulite on her legs, thereby resulting in my doing a mediocre backflip into a vat of self-pity and almond butter.

Most of the time it's because I'm taking myself way too damn seriously and have completely neglected doing anything fun for days or weeks or longer. Even when I've made it to this flavor of depression, my Logic is well aware of the importance of fun. I've seen it work magic in my life. However, when experiencing facial contortions due to sucking on the sour part of Life's Warhead candy, it becomes rather difficult to believe that there is any point *whatsoever* to fun or that the sweet part of the candy will ever arrive. It matters not how many times I've learned this lesson; I still struggle to incorporate it.

I am an analytical person, always wanting to know the *why.* Why am I sad today? Why am I so depressed? What did I do *wrong* to *deserve* this pain and suffering? I retrace my footsteps backwards in an effort to apply linear logic to something that mostly looks like this:

You know what this does?

It takes me away from the present moment. It has me mentally living in the past, *which doesn't even exist anymore,* trying to make logical sense of something that isn't at all logical. Mostly, it results in me doing a bunch of busy work that's about as useful as emptying my trash bin and organizing it all into piles. Ultimately, it's all going back into the trash bin. And situations from the past? They're going to stay in the past bin.

As with anything, I believe moderation plays a big part here. If I'm able to take a peek into my past and easily discern a situation or action (or inaction) that had a detrimental effect on my present, then so be it. The key, in my opinion, is that I:

A. Learn from it and return to the present moment.
B. Remove judgment rather than giving myself an unnecessarily hard time.

I could easily go Pro at giving myself a hard time. I have a tendency to micro-manage my life and apply unrealistic and unfair expectations for myself and others. I recognize that this is a mental program which has been running for a long time and will take effort to rewrite. In order to get to a place of light and love and butterflies and rainbows and gratitude, I need to make conscious effort in the present moment which reflects how I desire my reactions to be in the future.

What I mean is this: Right now is a down payment on the future. How I feel today is quite likely a result of what I paid forward from the past. There's no need to travel back there and try to "figure it out." Rather, the energy of this knowledge can be applied toward present-moment self-care. No matter how yucky I may feel, the action steps I take *now* are what will determine my moods of the future. Sure, sometimes hormones or sexy Starbucks patrons may throw me for a present-moment roller coaster ride, but overall, I believe this pay-it-forward mentality to be rather applicable.

It can certainly be difficult to get up and go for a walk or write a gratitude list when one is feeling downright lousy. It can feel *impossible.*

It is imperative that we **be kind to our future selves**. This requires being kind to our present selves, no matter how icky or un-motivated we feel. In the same way that unhealthy or unbeneficial actions aren't immediately felt, so too can it take time to feel the benefits of healthy choices.

One of the most important lessons I *keep learning* is that it's all about taking small, consistent steps. Small consistent steps are more sustainable than, say, my tendency to go from working out 0x per week to committing to working out AN HOUR PER DAY EVERY DAY NO MATTER WHAT. This drastic jump is a shock on the system and is difficult to maintain.

If I go from 0x per week to taking a few walks per week, however, it will become easier to increase and build activity from that point. Also, if each day's efforts are down payments on the future, the less extreme and more consistent choices will have a stable impact on the future rather than continuing the typical roller coaster ride.

~ * ~

I'm not 100% healed. I don't know if I ever will be. Or maybe I am and my level of awareness simply won't grasp it. Either way, my story is far from linear. In fact, it's rather messy. I'm rather messy. And that's *okay.* See, I initially used this as an excuse to not write. I believed I wasn't ______ enough. I wasn't aware enough or healed enough or emotionally stable enough. I wasn't *perfect* enough.

So now, whenever my Censor tries to say I'm not enough to write this book, my response is: *My only requirement is to be myself. Regardless of my mood or beliefs, I simply have to be myself and show up. Because that's the energy I want to put out into the world. Even when we feel uncomfortable or unsure or sad or mad, we are okay. We can utilize those feelings as fuel. So, Censor, although I appreciate your efforts to protect me, I am ready to take chances. I am ready to put myself out there. Yea, there will be rejection. There will also be acceptance. Most of all, there will be a ripple effect of other beautifully sensitive people beginning to travel into their cores so as to share their superpowers.*

Throughout this process, I kept acting *as if*. Even if I didn't feel as though I was sane enough or healed enough or successful enough to write this book, I utilized the energy to propel me forward and to act as if. When walking and meditating, I focused on what it would feel like to have completed the book. On more than one occasion, I acted out entire interviews with Ellen, in total expectation of being on her show.

Maybe I'm full of it, like my Censor says. Maybe this book will never get published. Maybe I'll never do a Ted Talk or be an inspirational speaker. Maybe I'll never be interviewed on Ellen. That's a possibility.

You know what else is a possibility? That the book will be published. I will do a Ted Talk. I will be an inspirational speaker. And I will dance with Ellen on her show.

Rather than focusing on what could go wrong, I instead choose to focus on what could go right. (I am in no way perfect with this mindset.) And, even if I die without any of these things being accomplished, I'll tell you one thing's for sure: it is *way more enjoyable* going through life believing in myself than not.

~ * ~

I'm not saying that awakening needs to look the way my journey has looked. I also am not saying "QUIT ALL DRUGS NOW!" I think there can be a time and place for medication. For me, it was a good temporary bridge during an extreme time of need. I don't believe I'd still be here today if I hadn't had access to anti-depressants during my darkest years.

Depression isn't something to fix. It isn't some knee scrape booboo in need of a little ointment and a Power Rangers Band-Aid. Depression is a state of being and can be a result of many things. It doesn't mean anything is *wrong* with you. It's an invitation. An invitation to dig deeper and embrace your sensitivities. Your feelings invite you to utilize their energy toward your passion. This is what brings life to life.

The moment I stopped treating my sensitivities like a curse and began embracing them as a potential blessing, my life transformed. I now utilize these gifts—which I used to call curses—to help others. These people, in turn, will use their gifts to guide others toward healing and awakening.

My argument is that this is why we are here. Our society is waking up and we each have been chosen to play a part in that awakening. The more sensitive we are, the larger impact we stand to have. And we don't have to be any more *anything* to begin working toward our dreams. As we take little action steps, our lives will begin delivering opportunities and support directly to us. One imperfect step at a time, our dreams will come true.

It is time to stop hiding.

I now give you permission to be imperfect.

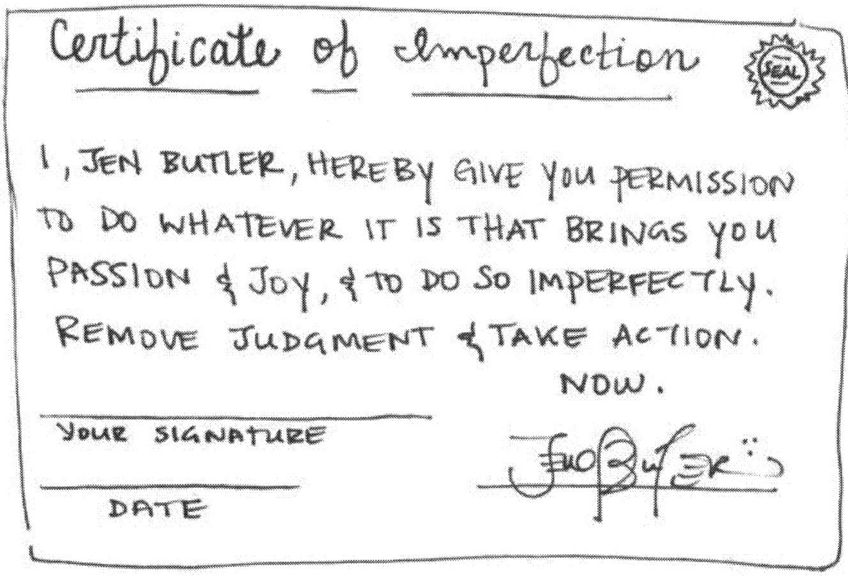

Certificate of Imperfection
SEAL
I, JEN BUTLER, HEREBY GIVE YOU PERMISSION TO DO WHATEVER IT IS THAT BRINGS YOU PASSION & JOY, & TO DO SO IMPERFECTLY.
REMOVE JUDGMENT & TAKE ACTION.
NOW.
YOUR SIGNATURE
DATE
Jen Butler :)

It is advisable to make a copy of this page and post it somewhere you will regularly see it.

LOVE NOTES TO FUTURE READERS

As a part of continuing and building upon the flow of this book, I ask that you give it to someone else. This can be someone you know. Or, if you fancy an adventure, place it in public. *Before passing this book on*, please take a moment to add to it. Use a small bit of space below to add words (and/or doodles) of wisdom or motivation for future readers. Do not put pressure on yourself about the "right" thing to write. Also, please don't be an ass-hat and write rude stuff; we deal with enough of that on a daily basis. Breathe into your heart and write whatever desires to come out. Perhaps imagine yourself at your lowest of lows. Or imagine if you were afraid to pursue your dream. What would you need to hear in that moment? Write it below. Then, pass this book along. Once you've done so? Scurry along and take some imperfect action.

What a GREAT idea! Thank you Jen for having the courage to write such an open honest autobiography. It takes a great deal of strength to be so vulnerable.

BE IMPERFECTLY YOU!!

We are all imperfect,
The MYTH of perfection
causes so much human
discomfort in so many ways
on so many levels.

pay it forward

You never know
when your act of
kindness might make
a huge difference.

... Somewhere between
the time you arrive
and the time you go
may lie a reason you
were alive that you'll
never know.
"FOR A DANCER"
Jackson Browne

WORDS OF ENCOURAGEMENT

When the power of LOVE becomes more important than the love of power Then we will have PEACE."

Jimi Hendrix

Love is not blind. Love sees more not less. And because it sees more, it is willing to see less!

Julius Gordon

You Rock.

HEY, FUTURE READER.
YOU'RE BUCKING FABULOUS.
KTHX. BYE.

Clucking honest book!
Thanx

Chuck the muck and keep on truckin'

We all puck up
It is part of being human.

I write from the heart

Please –
Take the time
to have FUN!

Give thanks for
unknown blessings
that are already
on the way

This is what
Support
looks like!

Was this book helpful for you? If you were one of the lucky folks who found a book in public and would like to show some monetary love, head to www.theimperfectbook.com to donate and/or share with others. This has been a labor of love and any help you give will be deeply appreciated.

My email address is jen@theimperfectbook.com. I'd love to hear from you, should you care to chat. If you're nice and/or funny and/or vulnerable, I'll respond. If you're rude, your email will be promptly fed to the junk box dragon.

Oh. Also. I've heard great things about this certain blog, www.jenniferannbutler.com. Maybe you should check it out and subscribe and share it with your friends. Just an idea.

also

@jenbutler.com

also

JenButler says

Look her up, her accomplishmen

are MANY.

ACCEPT THE CHALLENGE YOU ARE FACING. IT MAY BECOME YOUR GREATEST GIFT.

Jesus never claimed
to be perfect

Made in United States
Orlando, FL
07 August 2024

50077510R00124